IT TAKES A VILLAGE TO RAISE A CLASSROOM

BLACK FAMILY WISDOM IN EDUCATION

Dr. Krystal L. Clemons

IT TAKES A VILLAGE TO RAISE A CLASSROOM: BLACK
FAMILY WISDOM IN EDUCATION

Copyright © 2026 by KRYSTAL L. CLEMONS

ISBN: 9798245053882

Edited by Dr. Borbie L. Davis
Printed in the USA

DEDICATION

For the ancestors who taught us before schools ever did, for the families whose wisdom has too often been overlooked, and for the educators courageous enough to listen, learn, Moreover, build classrooms worthy of the village.

And always: for Eva and Imani.

TABLE OF CONTENTS

FOREWORD

I remember it as if it were yesterday. October 16, 1995…I attended the first Million Man March in Washington, D.C. Over one million Black men came together for an entire day on the mall, in a powerful show of unity, brotherhood, strength, and love. The day's culmination was a pledge taken in unison by all the men. The pledge was wide-ranging, but what stood out most to me was the commitment to return to our respective communities and do our part to make them better. I took that pledge quite seriously. I was a 5th grade teacher at the time in East Orange, NJ. When I got back to my school the next morning, I asked my principal if she would allow me to take all the boys in grades 3–5 outside after lunch to replicate my Million Man March experience. She obliged, and we all went outside that afternoon. The culminating activity was the recitation of a pledge I composed on the bus back to New Jersey the night before. What a powerful experience this was for the children, but for me, it lit a flame for how I can make my Million Man March experience an integral part of my leadership once I become a principal.

Two years later, I in fact became a principal. I immediately began building the program I had conceptualized while teaching 5th grade. A few years later, it was what I wanted it to be. It was called the Young Men's Empowerment Program, a direct product of and inspired by the Million Man March. In a nutshell, this was a program where, at the high school level, each Monday, I would take a different grade level of my young men out of class, and we would convene in my cafeteria or other large spaces for three to four hours. We would discuss everything under the sun to inform, inspire, and empower my young men. Additionally, on Mondays, which was the only day of the week that we had these meetings, my young men dressed as if they were the principal of the school…. shirt, tie, slacks, shoes, and a belt. However, as it relates to this book, the beauty of this program was who I brought in as speakers: the parents and community members…the village.

Dr. Clemons has titled this book *It Takes a Village to Raise a Classroom: Black Family Wisdom in Education.* I agree wholeheartedly, which is why I brought the parents and community as presenters with me. They came from a wide variety of experiential and professional backgrounds. They could therefore speak to the young men on a wide range of topics, preparing them for the world beyond school and supporting their success while they were in school. This particular school, Newark Tech HS in Newark, NJ, a CTE school, was the lowest performing school with the highest number of disciplinary referrals in my CTE district when I inherited it in 2005. By 2010, it was the highest performing school. I have long said that the Young Men's Empowerment Program played an immeasurable role in what Newark Tech accomplished during my tenure as principal. I might add that after my first year at Newark Tech, we expanded the program to include young women and called it the Young Women's Empowerment Program. We brought in so many women from the community and from our families…once again, the village.

The success of Newark Tech and the success of the Young Men's & Young Women's Empowerment Program were inseparable, and at the heart of both was the role of the parents and community…the village that Dr. Clemons so powerfully speaks to throughout this phenomenal must-read book. I am convinced beyond the shadow of a doubt that schools, particularly schools serving the needs of historically underserved student populations in general and historically underserved Black children in particular, cannot perform at optimal levels as presently constructed without the arms of the village wrapped around them. Because the school is in the heart of the community, the community must be embraced as an integral part of the educational process. The community, parents, and the village cannot be viewed as separate from the schoolhouse. They need each other. They should be viewed as one. The school needs the village, and the village needs the school to perform at high levels to sustain the village. This partnership can never be underestimated. The difference between a child's success and failure could be rooted in this relationship. I do not believe schools can do the heavy lifting of properly educating children alone or in a vacuum. The village's role is essential and immeasurable.

PRINCIPAL BARUTI KAFELE
RETIRED PRINCIPAL, EDUCATION CONSULTANT, AUTHOR

PREFACE

I come from a family of educators. Long before I entered a classroom as a professional, education was already part of my lineage. It appeared in conversations at family gatherings and church services, in stories about students who stayed late or returned years later, and in the deep sense of responsibility my relatives felt for children who were not their biological children but were treated as if they were. Teaching was never just a job in my family—it was a calling, a commitment, and a collective act of care.

In my family, education was not confined to schools. It lived in expectations, accountability, encouragement, and love. It lived in the belief that every child belonged to all of us and that our role as adults was not only to instruct but also to nurture, protect, and prepare. These lessons were not taught through formal curriculum, but through modeling— through watching educators pour themselves into classrooms during the day and still show up for their communities in the evenings.

As I moved through my own professional journey as an educator, school counselor, consultant, and scholar, I began to recognize a troubling contradiction. The very values I had grown up seeing modeled—collective responsibility, deep relationships, cultural knowledge—were often absent from how schools engaged Black families. Too often, family engagement was reduced to attendance, compliance, or visibility, while families' lived expertise was minimized or ignored. Black families, including those who were educators themselves, were positioned as participants on the margins rather than partners at the center. This book was written in response to that contradiction.

It Takes a Village to Raise a Classroom: Black Family Wisdom in Education is grounded in what my family—and so many Black families— have always known: that education is relational, intergenerational, and communal. Long before engagement frameworks existed, Black educators and families taught children to navigate institutions, advocate for themselves, and carry themselves with dignity in spaces not built for them. That wisdom has sustained generations, even when systems fail to recognize it.

Throughout this book, I draw from research, professional practice, and lived experience to challenge deficit-based narratives and offer a reimagined vision of school–family partnership. I ask educators and school leaders to move beyond transactional engagement and toward relationships rooted in trust, respect, and shared responsibility. I invite readers to see families not as obstacles to manage or audiences to inform, but as co-educators whose knowledge is essential to student success.

This book is written for educators, school counselors, administrators, mental-health professionals, and community partners who understand that something deeper is required. It is for those who recognize that equity cannot exist without relationship, and that meaningful change begins when we listen to the wisdom already present in our communities.

My family taught me that education is never an individual effort—it is a shared one. The village does not begin at the school doors, and it does not end when the bell rings. This book is both a reflection of that truth and an invitation to honor it.

INTRODUCTION

An old African proverb whispers this fundamental truth: it takes a village to raise a child. However, what happens when that village decides to raise a classroom? What magic unfolds when an entire community turns its collective wisdom, strength, and love toward education? In Black communities, learning has never been confined to four walls or a single teacher's desk. It is a living, breathing ecosystem that extends from front porches to church basements, from family reunions to neighborhood block parties. Every adult is a potential teacher, every experience a potential lesson, every struggle a potential curriculum. When Ms. Johnson from down the street notices a child struggling with reading, she doesn't just pass by. She pulls out the books her own children loved, sits down on the stoop, and creates a moment of learning. When the local barber shop becomes a Saturday morning classroom where young men learn about history, mathematics, and self-worth between haircuts, that's the village at work. When grandmothers teach cooking as a lesson in chemistry, measurement, and cultural preservation, that's the village raising not just a child, but a whole classroom of understanding.

Our village not only supplements education but fundamentally reimagines it. We know that learning is not a linear path but a circular journey. Knowledge doesn't flow in one direction from teacher to student, but it circles around, enriched by every voice, every experience, every generational story. This village approach means no child is ever truly alone in their learning. When one struggles, multiple hands reach out. When one succeeds, the entire community celebrates. We understand that education is not about individual achievement, but collective elevation. A child's report card is not just a reflection of their effort but also a testament to the countless hands that have guided, supported, and believed in them.

Although this book centers the brilliance, care, and ingenuity of Black families, it does not ignore the realities that have made such collective strategies necessary. Schools in the United States were not created in neutral contexts; they developed within racial hierarchies that have long positioned Black children as deficient, threatening, or less deserving of full educational investment—a pattern traced in foundational educational histories (Anderson, 1988) and later theorized through critical race frameworks that continue to shape contemporary schooling (Ladson-Billings, 1998). More recently, scholars have conceptualized anti-Blackness as a structural condition embedded in policies, practices, and cultural narratives that influence discipline, curriculum, academic expectations, and access to opportunity (Dumas, 2016; Kendi, 2016; Love, 2019; Morris, 2016). Naming these conditions is not an act of despair but of clarity. It allows us to better understand why families build villages around their children, why preparation becomes ritual, and why community wisdom functions not as an accessory to schooling but as a necessary form of protection, affirmation, and advocacy.

In our classrooms—whether in schools, community centers, or makeshift learning spaces—we are not just teaching subjects; we are teaching survival, resilience, identity, and possibility. We are showing our children that they come from a long line of brilliant, creative problem-solvers, and that their learning is an act of both personal growth and community healing. The village does not just raise the child; it raises the entire classroom—transforming education from a system into a living, breathing community of care, challenge, and infinite potential.

This is our story. This is our learning.

CHAPTER ONE: ROOTS OF RESILIENCE

"Know from whence you came. If you know whence you came, there are absolutely no limitations to where you can go."
— **James Baldwin**

The old church basement smelled of coffee and chalk dust, the kind of place where knowledge had been passed down for generations through whispered lessons and borrowed textbooks. Miss Johnson, all of eighty-three years old, sat at the head of the long folding table, her weathered hands smoothing the pages of a worn primer. Around her, children from the neighborhood leaned in close, hungry for the words she offered like daily bread. "Learning," she would say, adjusting her glasses and looking each child in the eye, "is sacred work. Don't let anybody tell you different." This scene, repeated in countless communities across America, speaks to a truth that runs deeper than policy papers and standardized tests. In Black families and communities, education has never been merely about grades or graduation rates. It was about survival, dignity, and the audacious act of claiming our rightful place in a world that too often said we didn't belong.

The Sacred Nature of Learning

To understand the depth of Black families' commitment to education, we must first understand what learning has meant to our people. From the moment enslaved Africans were forbidden to read under penalty of death (Anderson, 1988), literacy became more than a skill—it became an act of resistance, a pathway to freedom, and a sacred trust between generations. The kitchen table became our first classroom. The front porch is our laboratory for life lessons. The church sanctuary is our university of moral education (Lincoln & Mamiya, 1990). These weren't substitutes for "real" education; they were the foundation upon which all meaningful learning would build.

Consider the grandmother who taught multiplication tables while braiding hair, her fingers working in rhythm with numbers that would unlock doors her own education had been denied. Think of the father who turned every car ride into a vocabulary lesson, believing that words were weapons against ignorance and armor against discrimination. Remember the mother who stayed up past midnight helping with homework she had never had the chance to complete herself, determined that her child would walk through doors that had been closed to her. This is the sacred nature of learning in Black families—education as liberation, knowledge as inheritance, and wisdom as the most precious gift we can pass down.

Survival, Hope, and Knowledge as Inheritance

Our ancestors understood something that modern educational reform often misses: knowledge without context is powerless, but knowledge rooted in purpose can move mountains. They knew that their children would face a world designed to diminish them, so they armed them not just with facts and figures, but with the strength to persevere, the wisdom to navigate, and the hope to transcend. The stories passed down through generations weren't just entertainment—they were survival manuals. The tale of the enslaved who learned to read by tracing letters in the dirt became a lesson about finding opportunity in the most unlikely places. The grandmother's account of walking miles to a one-room schoolhouse became a testament to the value of persistence. The narrative of the first in the family to graduate from college became proof that barriers could be broken and dreams achieved. These stories carried within them the accumulated wisdom of survival: how to code-switch between home and school languages, how to excel without threatening fragile egos, how to maintain dignity in the face of discrimination, and how to use education as a tool for not just personal advancement but for uplifting the community.

The inheritance was complex—part caution, part courage. "Work twice as hard to get half as much," parents would warn, but in the same breath, they'd add, "But never let that stop you from reaching for everything." This wasn't contradictory; it was preparation for a reality that demanded both excellence and resilience.

Stories That Shape Our Educational Journey

Every Black family has them: the stories that become legend, the moments that define our relationship with learning, the people who embodied the transformative power of education. These narratives are not always about traditional academic success. Sometimes they're about the uncle who could not read but possessed a wisdom that guided the whole family. Other times they're about the sister who left school to work but never stopped learning, turning every experience into a lesson for those who came after.

There is power in these stories because they remind us that education isn't confined to classroom walls or limited to certain ages. They teach us that intelligence comes in many forms, that wisdom can be found in unexpected places, and that the most important learning often happens in the spaces between formal lessons. The young mother who reads bedtime stories with exaggerated voices, bringing characters to life and sparking imagination. The grandfather who turns grocery shopping into lessons about budgeting, nutrition, and community economics. The teenage brother who explains algebra using basketball statistics, making abstract concepts concrete and relevant. These are the educators who rarely receive recognition but shape young minds in profound ways.

These family educators understood intuitively what research now confirms: children learn best when education connects to their lived experiences, when knowledge is presented with love and high expectations, and when learning is seen as a community endeavor rather than an individual competition (Nasir et al, 2019; Nasir et al., 2020).

The Village in the Classroom

The African proverb "It takes a whole village to raise a child" finds its most powerful expression in how Black families approach education. The village isn't just geographical—it's philosophical. It's the understanding that every child's success strengthens the whole community, and every child's failure diminishes us all. This village mentality espoused the philosophy that education was never left solely to schools. Parents, grandparents, aunts, uncles, neighbors, and church members all saw themselves as teachers: The barber who quizzed children on their spelling while cutting their hair. The beautician who discussed current events while styling hair. The deacon who expected perfect recitation of scriptures and poetry alike; they all understood their role in the collective work of raising educated, principled young people.

The village also provided multiple models of success and different pathways to achievement. Children could see themselves in the teacher who looked like them, the doctor who grew up in their neighborhood, the entrepreneur who started with nothing but determination. These weren't distant celebrities but real people with familiar stories, proving that excellence was possible and accessible.

Wisdom for Today's Educators

As we navigate the complexities of modern education, the resilience-planting roots of previous generations offer invaluable guidance. The sacred nature of learning reminds us that education is about more than test scores and college admission rates: it is about developing the whole child, representing our children, honoring their cultural wealth (Yosso, 2005), and preparing them to be agents of positive change in their communities. The tradition of survival, hope, and knowledge as inheritance teaches us that education must be both rigorous and relevant, challenging students academically while connecting to their cultural experiences and community needs. It shows us that high expectations and warm support aren't contradictory but complementary (Nasir et al, 2019; Nasir et al., 2020).

The power of stories that shape our educational journey reminds us that narrative matters, that representation counts, and that our children need to see themselves reflected in the curriculum and in the adults who teach them. These roots of resilience do not just belong to Black families—they offer wisdom for all educators who understand that teaching is about more than delivering content. Wise educators work diligently to create conditions where every child can thrive, where learning is joyful and meaningful, and where education serves as a bridge to a better future for individuals and communities alike. The sacred work continues. In every classroom where a teacher sees potential instead of deficits, in every family that prioritizes learning over convenience, in every community that invests in its children's future. The roots run deep, and from them, new growth emerges—stronger, wiser, and more resilient than ever before.

The village that raised us now calls us to raise the next generation. The question isn't whether we're capable—our ancestors proved that. The question is whether we're willing to honor their legacy by continuing the sacred work of education, one child, one family, one classroom at a time.

"Return to the root and you will find the meaning." - **Sengcan**

CHAPTER TWO: THE VILLAGE THAT RAISES LEARNERS

"The children are always ours, every single one of them, all over the globe; and I am beginning to suspect that whoever is incapable of recognizing this may be incapable of morality."
— **James Baldwin**

Seven-year-old Marcus was struggling with fractions, the numbers swimming on the page like mysterious codes he couldn't crack. His mother had tried everything—flashcards, online videos, even bribing him with his favorite candy. Nothing worked. Then one Saturday afternoon at his grandmother's house, Uncle Jerome sat down at the kitchen table with a deck of cards and a pizza. "Boy, you hungry?" Uncle Jerome asked, dealing cards with practiced ease. "Good, 'cause we bout to learn fractions the real way." For the next hour, pizza slices became denominators, card suits became numerators, and suddenly fractions weren't abstract concepts but tools for fair sharing and strategic thinking. By dinner time, Marcus was teaching his younger cousins what he'd learned, his confidence rebuilt through the patient teaching of an uncle who'd never set foot in a classroom but understood how learning really happens.

This is the village at work—not as metaphor, but as living reality. In Black communities, education has never been confined to the nuclear family or limited to certified teachers (Clemons, 2024; Nasir et al., 2020). It flows through networks of care that extend far beyond blood relations, creating webs of wisdom that catch falling children and lift them toward success (Clemons, 2024).

Beyond Nuclear Families: Community as Classroom

The traditional nuclear family model, while important, tells only part of the story of how Black children learn and thrive. In our communities, the boundaries of family stretch to include chosen relatives, longtime neighbors, church members, and anyone who takes a genuine interest in a child's development (Nasir et al., 2019). This expansive definition of family creates multiple safety nets and numerous opportunities for learning (Jeynes, 2016).

The barbershop--where young boys learn not just about grooming but about manhood, respect, and community pride. The barber remembers every child's name and grade level, who asks about report cards between haircuts, and who celebrates achievements with high-fives and words of encouragement. This isn't just small talk: it is accountability wrapped in care, expectations delivered with love. Or think about the beauty salon where girls absorb lessons about self-worth, financial literacy, and professional behavior while they and their mothers get their hair done. The stylists who ask about school projects, offer advice about friend drama, and share stories of their own educational journeys. These women become mentors without formal titles, teachers without lesson plans, but educators nonetheless: the corner store owner who knows which children are honor roll students and which ones need extra encouragement. The church secretary who types up scholarship applications for free. The retired teacher who tutors neighborhood kids at her kitchen table every Tuesday and Thursday. These aren't random acts of kindness—they're expressions of a deep cultural understanding that every child's success strengthens the entire community (Love, 2019; Clemons, 2024).

This expanded classroom model recognizes that children learn differently and need different kinds of support at different times (Nasir et al., 2020). Some children thrive with their parents' help but struggle with peer pressure—the cool older cousin who makes academic success seem achievable becomes crucial. Others need the repetition that comes from a grandmother who has all day and all the love in the world. Still others require the tough love of an uncle who won't accept excuses but will stay up all night helping with a science project or an English literary analysis of character.

Aunties, Uncles, Elders as Unexpected Teachers

In Black families, the terms "auntie" and "uncle" stretch far beyond biological relationships. They're titles of respect and recognition that acknowledge the special role certain adults play in children's lives (Yosso, 2005). These chosen family members often become some of the most influential teachers a child will ever have (Clemons, 2024).

Auntie Sarah might not have finished high school herself, but she has a library of life experiences that rival any textbook. She teaches patience through her detailed stories, problem-solving through her resourcefulness, and resilience through her own journey of overcoming obstacles. When she sits down to help with homework, she brings more than academic knowledge: she brings perspective, encouragement, and the absolute belief that this child can succeed. Uncle Robert, the family mechanic, transforms his garage into a laboratory where nephews and neighborhood kids learn about physics through engine repair, chemistry through understanding how different fluids interact, and mathematics through calculating measurements and costs. His grease-stained hands are more effective than any science teacher's pristine demonstrations because they show learning in action, knowledge applied to real-world problems.

These unexpected teachers often succeed where traditional educators struggle because they understand the child's full context. They know the family dynamics, the neighborhood challenges, and the cultural references that make learning stick. They can switch between standard English and home dialect seamlessly, translating concepts across cultural codes in ways that feel natural rather than forced. The silver-headed elderly woman the street who survived segregation and integration brings historical perspective that no textbook can match. Her stories about walking past angry crowds to enter all-white schools aren't just history lessons—they're master classes in courage, determination, and the transformative power of education. When she tells children about the price paid for their educational opportunities, they understand viscerally why their success matters.

These community educators often specialize in lessons that formal schools struggle to teach: the grandmother who insists on proper pronunciation and grammar, understanding that code-switching is survival skill; the church deacon who connects Bible stories to moral decision-making and character development; and, the neighbor who teaches children how to garden, showing them the connection between patience, nurturing, and growth that applies to both plants and academic achievement.

Wisdom that Flows Through Generations

The most powerful aspect of the village educational model is that wisdom flows in multiple directions, not just from older to younger, in continuous cycles that enrich everyone involved. Children learn from elders, but elders also learn from children. Teenagers mentor younger kids while receiving guidance from adults. Knowledge becomes a currency that circulates throughout the community, growing stronger with each exchange.

This generational flow creates unique learning opportunities that formal education often misses. The grandmother teaching traditional recipes is not just passing on cooking skills; she is also sharing lessons about measurement, chemistry, cultural heritage, and family history. Teenagers showing an elder how to use a smartphone is more than just providing tech support; it is about practicing patience, developing teaching skills, and building intergenerational bridges.

The wisdom that flows through these generational exchanges often carries profound life lessons embedded in everyday activities: the grandfather who teaches chess on the front porch is not just explaining the rules; he is also demonstrating strategic thinking, the importance of considering consequences before acting, and how to remain calm under pressure. These lessons stick because they are learned through relationship, reinforced through repetition, and applied in real contexts.

Stories become the vessels through which wisdom travels between generations. The tale of Great-Grandmother's journey north during the Great Migration carries lessons about courage, adaptability, and the importance of education as a pathway to better opportunities. The account of the uncle who started his own business after being passed over for promotions teaches entrepreneurship, persistence, and the value of taking calculated risks.

Rather than being mere entertainment, these stories become oral textbooks that contain survival strategies, moral guidance, and aspirational blueprints; they teach children that they come from people who overcame impossible odds, valued learning above material possessions, and believed in investing in the next generation even when resources were scarce.

The flow of wisdom from these stories also includes practical knowledge often overlooked by formal education: practice knowledge like how to budget when money is tight, how to navigate predominantly white institutions while maintaining cultural identity, how to turn setbacks into comebacks, and finally, how to use education as a tool for uplifting the community rather than just individual advancement.

The Multiplier Effect

When a village truly commits to raising learners, the impact multiplies exponentially. One child's success inspires siblings, cousins, and neighbors. One family's commitment to education raises the expectations for entire blocks. One community's investment in its children transforms neighborhoods and breaks cycles of limited opportunity.

This multiplier effect happens because village-raised learners understand from early age that their education is not just about personal achievement; instead, it is about community advancement as they are carrying the hopes and dreams of multiple generations, the sacrifices of ancestors, and the expectations of a community that has invested in their success. This weight could be crushing, but when properly supported by the village, it becomes motivating rather than burdensome. The multiplier effect has concrete manifestations clearly seen in the child who succeeds becomes a role model for younger children, proving that achievement is possible and providing a roadmap for others to follow; the teenager who gets a scholarship returns to share knowledge about college applications and financial aid; and, the college graduate comes back to mentor high school students, creating cycles of support that strengthen with each generation.

These success stories become part of the community's narrative, adding to the collection of wisdom that flows through generations. They provide concrete examples of what's possible while acknowledging the challenges that must be overcome. They celebrate achievement while remaining grounded in the understanding that individual success is meaningless without community progress.

Modern Applications of Ancient Wisdom

Today's educators and families can learn valuable lessons from the village model of raising learners. These lessons reveal recognition that learning happens everywhere, that every adult has something valuable to teach, and that children thrive when surrounded by multiple sources of support and high expectations. Schools that embrace the village concept create partnerships with community members, inviting local entrepreneurs, artists, and elders to share their expertise with students. They recognize parents and community members as co-educators rather than obstacles to overcome (Warren et al., 2009; Milner, 2020). They understand that cultural wealth exists in every community, and they work to build bridges between home and school knowledge.

Families that operate from the village mindset seek out mentors and role models for their children, understanding that different adults can provide different kinds of support and inspiration. They reciprocate by mentoring other children, recognizing that community investment creates community returns.

The village model also underscores the importance of intergenerational relationships in education. Too often, we segregate learning by age, missing out on the rich exchanges that occur when different generations learn together. The wisdom of elders, the energy of youth, and the bridge-building capacity of middle generations all contribute to comprehensive educational experiences.

Challenges and Solutions

The village model faces real challenges in modern society. Geographic mobility separates families. Economic pressures limit time for community engagement. While technology offers new learning opportunities, it can also create barriers to traditional relationship-building. Yet innovative communities find ways to maintain village connections even in changed circumstances. Virtual mentoring programs connect elders with young people across distances. Community centers have become gathering places where different generations can interact around shared learning goals. Schools create family engagement programs that honor community members' expertise while building educational partnerships. The key is intentionally creating opportunities for the kind of natural learning exchanges that once happened automatically in more connected communities. This might mean organizing skill-sharing events where community members teach what they know, creating mentorship programs that pair children with caring adults, or simply encouraging the kind of informal educational conversations that happen when adults take genuine interest in children's lives.

The Continuing Legacy

The village that raises learners does more than produce individual success stories: it creates cultures of learning that persist across generations; it builds communities where education is valued, where knowledge is shared freely, and where every child knows they have multiple people invested in their success. This legacy continues today in communities that understand the power of collective responsibility for children's education. It lives in the programs that bring elders into schools to share their wisdom, the initiatives that train community members to serve as tutors and mentors, and the families who open their homes to neighborhood children who need additional support. The village model reminds us that education is fundamentally a social endeavor, that learning happens best in the context of caring relationships, and that wisdom flows most freely when we create multiple pathways for its transmission (Love, 2019). It teaches us that every adult is a potential teacher, every child is a potential learner, and every community has the resources needed to raise learners who will change the world.

"Each one teach one" isn't just a slogan: it is a blueprint for educational transformation that begins with recognizing the village that already exists and empowering it to do what it has always done best: raise learners who carry the wisdom of generations into an ever-changing future.

"The most important thing we learn at school is the fact that the most important things can't be learned at school." – **Haruki Murakami**

CHAPTER THREE: CULTURAL WEALTH IN OUR FAMILIES

"Wealth is also defined by family, connection to our ancestry, and our best vision of the future." – **Nainoa Thompson**

Ten-year-old Keisha sat in the principal's office, her eyes downcast as the adults around her discussed her "behavior problems." The teacher complained about her "argumentative nature" and "failure to follow instructions." The counselor mentioned concerns about "defiance" and suggested testing for learning disabilities. No one seemed to notice that Keisha wasn't defiant; she was translating. When the teacher said, "Turn to page forty-seven," Keisha automatically looked around to make sure her classmate Jayden, who struggled with reading, had found the right page. When asked to work quietly, she whispered encouragement to students who seemed frustrated. When the teacher asked a question, she waited to see if others wanted to answer first, having been taught at home that taking up too much space was impolite.

These were not behavior problems; they were leadership skills, community consciousness, and cultural values in action. But in a system that didn't recognize cultural wealth, Keisha's strengths were being reframed as deficits, her assets dismissed as obstacles. This scene plays out in schools across America every day, where Black children's cultural wealth—defined by Dr. Tara Yosso (2005) as the rich collection of knowledge, skills, abilities, and contacts accumulated through living and persisting in marginalized communities—is often invisible to educators trained to see only traditional academic markers of success, completely blind to the powerful dynamics and insights of cultural awareness that would them more effective educators.

The Strengths We Bring into Learning Spaces

Black families enter education carrying treasure chests of cultural wealth accumulated over generations of survival, resistance, and triumph (Clemons, 2024; Nasir et al., 2020). This wealth is not measured in bank accounts or test scores. Rather, it is embedded in ways of thinking, patterns of interaction, and approaches to problem-solving that have enabled communities to thrive against incredible odds.

Aspirational Capital. Aspirational capital flows through families like a river of hope. It's the grandmother who never finished high school but insists her grandchildren will attend college. It's the single mother working three jobs who still finds time to quiz her son on vocabulary words because she believes education will open doors that were closed to her. This isn't naive optimism—it's strategic hope based on a deep understanding that education, despite its flaws, remains one of the most reliable pathways to opportunity (Yosso, 2005; Jeynes, 2016). Aspirational capital in Black families often carries a multigenerational perspective that extends far beyond individual achievement. Parents speak not just of their children's success but of breaking cycles, lifting the whole family, and creating opportunities for generations yet unborn. This long-term vision creates a sense of purpose that motivates students through difficult times and helps them understand that their education serves something larger than personal advancement.

Linguistic Capital. Linguistic capital manifests in the sophisticated code-switching abilities that Black children develop naturally. They navigate between home language and school language, formal presentations and playground conversations, Sunday morning church speak, and weekday classroom discussions. This isn't confusion; instead, it is linguistic dexterity that demonstrates cognitive flexibility and cultural competence. Essentially, the child who can translate complex ideas into language their younger sibling understands, who can explain the same concept to their grandmother and their teacher using different vocabularies, who can move seamlessly between different communication styles depending on context—this child possesses linguistic capital that represents advanced communication skills often unrecognized by traditional assessment tools.

Familial Capital. Familial capital shows up in the deep understanding of kinship networks, collective responsibility, and intergenerational support that characterizes Black family structures. Children who help raise younger siblings are not just babysitting—they're developing teaching skills, learning patience, and understanding developmental psychology in practical ways. Students who translate for non-English-speaking family members are developing interpretation skills and cultural bridge-building abilities. The teenager who manages the family budget while mom works overtime is not being robbed of childhood because they are benefiting educationally by developing financial literacy, organizational skills, and understanding of economic systems that will serve them throughout life. Likewise, the child who mediates family conflicts is not being burdened inappropriately; rather, he or she is gaining invaluable knowledge by learning negotiation skills, empathy, and conflict-resolution strategies.

Social Capital. Social capital emerges from the networks of support, information sharing, and mutual aid that sustain Black communities. Children learn early how to build relationships across differences, how to seek help when needed, and how to aid others. They understand that individual success is meaningless without community uplift, and they develop skills in collaboration and collective problem-solving. The student who knows which adults in their neighborhood are safe to approach for help, who can navigate different social contexts with appropriate behavior, who understands how to build alliances and advocate for themselves and others—this student possesses social capital that represents a sophisticated understanding of human relationships and social systems.

Navigational Capital. Navigational capital represents the skills developed through navigating hostile environments and institutions. Black children often develop exceptional abilities to read social situations, assess potential threats and opportunities, and adjust their behavior accordingly. They learn to persist through discouragement, to find alternative pathways when direct routes are blocked, and to maintain dignity in the face of disrespect. The student who can sense when a teacher has lowered expectations and responds by working harder to prove their capability demonstrates navigational capital. The child who finds ways to get extra help without appearing needy, who builds relationships with adults who can open doors, who persists through setbacks while maintaining optimism—these skills represent sophisticated survival intelligence.

Resistant Capital. Resistant Capital flows from the legacy of resistance to oppression and the knowledge accumulated through challenging injustice. This capital shows up in students who question unfair practices, who speak up for classmates being treated poorly, and who maintain pride in their identity even when it's devalued by others. Far from being "troublemakers," these students are exercising critical thinking and moral courage—both vital aspects of resistant capital.

Turning Our Lived Experiences into Educational Power

The key to unlocking cultural wealth in educational settings lies in recognizing how lived experiences can be transformed into learning assets rather than obstacles to overcome. This requires a fundamental shift in perspective: from deficit thinking that asks, "What are these students lacking?" to asset-based thinking that asks, "What strengths are these students bringing?" which ultimately translates into educational power.

Storytelling as an Academic Skill. In many Black families, storytelling is more than just entertainment; it is education. Children learn to construct narratives, understand character development, recognize cause and effect, and communicate complex ideas through story. When educators recognize these storytelling abilities as sophisticated communication skills, they can build upon them to develop academic writing, public speaking, and analytical thinking. Thus, the child who can hold an audience captive with a detailed account of their weekend adventures possesses narrative skills that can be channeled into essay writing, creative projects, and oral presentations. The student who naturally includes dialogue, sensory details, and emotional resonance in their stories already understands elements of effective communication that many students struggle to master.

Problem-Solving Through Resource Creativity. Growing up in communities where resources are often limited teaches children to be innovative problem-solvers. They learn to make something from nothing, to find multiple uses for single items, and to think creatively about solutions. These aren't just survival skills—they're design thinking capabilities that can revolutionize approaches to academic challenges. The student, therefore, who can create a science project using materials from around the house demonstrates resourcefulness and creativity. The child who finds three different ways to solve a math problem because they've learned that there's always another approach when the first one doesn't work shows mathematical flexibility and persistence.

Leadership Through Service. Many Black children grow up understanding that leadership means service to the community. They learn to take care of others before themselves, to step up when help is needed, and to use their abilities to lift others. When educators recognize these service orientations as leadership skills, they can channel them into peer tutoring, group project management, and community service learning, allowing them to see the big picture. They then understand that students who automatically help struggling classmates do not constitute cheating or being disruptive. Instead, they are demonstrating collaborative leadership skills. Students who take responsibility for ensuring everyone understands the assignment demonstrate project management skills and inclusive thinking.

Cultural Translation Skills. Black children often serve as cultural bridges, helping family members navigate predominantly white institutions while maintaining their cultural identity. This develops sophisticated skills in reading context, adapting communication styles, and building relationships across differences. Ultimately, the student who can explain school expectations to parents while helping parents' perspectives make sense to teachers demonstrates cultural competency that's invaluable in our increasingly diverse society. The child who maintains respect for diverse cultural values while functioning effectively across various settings demonstrates diplomatic skills and emotional intelligence.

Redefining Intelligence Beyond Traditional Metrics. Traditional measures of intelligence, like standardized tests, grade point averages, and SAT scores, capture only a narrow slice of human capability. They, however, often miss the sophisticated thinking skills, emotional intelligence, and creative problem-solving abilities that Black children develop through their cultural experiences. Black children demonstrate an impressive range of intelligences which are often unrecognized and overlooked.

Collective Intelligence vs Individual Competition. Many Black children are raised with values that prioritize group success over individual achievement. They learn to share resources, collaborate on solutions, and measure success by how well the whole group performs. In educational settings that value only individual competition, these collaborative orientations can be misread as cheating or a lack of independent thinking. But collective intelligence represents a sophisticated understanding of how real-world problems are solved. The most complex challenges facing society—from climate change to technological innovation—require collaborative solutions. Students who naturally think in terms of "How can we all succeed?" rather than "How can I beat everyone else?" possess collaborative intelligence that's increasingly valuable.

Emotional and Social Intelligence. Black children often also develop exceptional abilities to read social situations, understand emotional undercurrents, and navigate complex interpersonal dynamics. They learn to assess whether adults are trustworthy, to sense when situations are becoming unsafe, and to adjust their behavior to protect themselves and others. These emotional intelligence skills show up as a sophisticated understanding of human behavior, the ability to build relationships across differences, and the capacity to mediate conflicts. Students who can sense when a classmate is struggling emotionally and know how to offer appropriate support demonstrate empathy and social awareness that are crucial life skills.

Creative and Artistic Intelligence. Apart from emotional and social intelligence, Black cultural traditions are rich with creative expression from musical improvisation to visual storytelling to dance as communication, giving Black kids creative and artistic intelligence that translates into insights and abilities beyond their years. Thus, children exposed to these traditions often develop sophisticated aesthetic sensibilities, creative problem-solving abilities, and an understanding of how art can convey complex messages. Black children demonstrate their artistic and creative intelligence in their unique ability in these ways: by the student who can freestyle rap demonstrates linguistic creativity, rhythm, and ability to think quickly under pressure; by the child who can create elaborate hairstyles shows spatial intelligence, aesthetic sense, and fine motor skills; and by the teenager who can DJ at family gatherings understands music theory, crowd psychology, and event management.

Spiritual Intelligence. Raised with strong spiritual foundations that teach them to see beyond immediate circumstances, to maintain hope in difficult times, and to understand their place in larger cosmic purposes, Black children naturally display spiritual intelligence. This spiritual intelligence manifests as resilience, moral reasoning, and the ability to find meaning in struggle. Students who can maintain optimism despite facing discrimination demonstrate psychological resilience. They essentially become individuals who make moral decisions based on principles rather than peer pressure, show ethical reasoning, and understand that their individual success serves larger purposes, and possess motivational intelligence that sustains long-term effort.

Survival Intelligence. Forced by a society that pushes them to navigate marginalized status, students develop survival intelligence skills—hypervigilance, strategic thinking, and quick assessments of risks and opportunities. Black children display sophisticated survival intelligence skills that translate into academic and professional settings. The student who can quickly assess which teachers have high expectations and which have given up demonstrates social intelligence, the child who knows how to advocate for themselves without appearing threatening shows strategic communication skills, and the teenager who can maintain cultural pride while succeeding in predominantly white environments demonstrates identity management abilities, all embody and reveal their survival intelligence skills.

Practical Applications in Educational Settings

Recognizing cultural wealth requires educators to fundamentally shift their approaches to assessment, instruction, and relationship-building with students and families using a variety of practical methods.

Asset-Based Assessment. Instead of focusing only on what students cannot do, educators can create assessment tools that reveal what students can do. These might include portfolios that highlight diverse talents, project-based assessments that allow for creative problem-solving, and evaluation methods that recognize collaborative skills alongside individual achievement.

Culturally Responsive Pedagogy. Culturally responsive pedagogy focuses on teaching that builds upon students' cultural wealth and connects new learning to existing knowledge and experiences. This might mean using hip-hop to teach poetry structure, incorporating family stories into history lessons, or allowing students to demonstrate learning through culturally familiar formats.

Family Partnership Models. Family partnership models, such as the Village Model of Community Engagement© (Clemons, 2024), show that schools that recognize families' cultural wealth create genuine partnerships rather than one-way communication. These schools invite family members to share their expertise, they honor different communication styles, and they recognize that parents are the child's first and most important teachers.

Strength-Based Student Support. Strength-based student support differs from worn-out remediation strategies that focus only on overcoming weaknesses. Support services can build upon student strengths while addressing areas for growth. This approach might mean pairing students who excel in creative expression with students who excel in analytical thinking or creating leadership opportunities that channel students' natural collaborative abilities.

The Transformation Imperative

Educational effectiveness extends beyond recognizing and building upon cultural wealth. It is not just about being nice to students or making them feel better about themselves. Educational effectiveness must be driving or central for all that is done. In fact, when schools tap into the sophisticated thinking skills, creative abilities, and problem-solving strategies that students bring from their cultural experiences, learning accelerates dramatically. Moreover, students who see their cultural wealth valued in school become more engaged, more confident, and more willing to take academic risks. They understand that education builds on their existing strengths rather than replacing their cultural identity. They see school as an extension of their community's values rather than a rejection of them.

The student whose storytelling abilities are recognized and developed becomes a powerful writer. The child whose collaborative skills are valued becomes an effective leader. The teenager whose survival intelligence is honored becomes a strategic thinker. The transformation happens not through deficit remediation but through strength amplification (Love, 2019; Nasir et al., 2020).

This shift requires courage from educators, families, and communities. It means challenging systems that have historically devalued Black cultural wealth. It means insisting that intelligence is multifaceted, that strength comes in many forms, and that every child brings valuable assets to the learning process. But the rewards are transformational—not just for individual students, but for educational systems that become richer, more effective, and more equitable when they embrace the full range of human intelligence and cultural wisdom that students bring to learning.

The cultural wealth in Black families represents generations of accumulated wisdom, survival strategies, creative solutions, and collective knowledge. When educational systems learn to see this wealth rather than focusing on perceived deficits, they unlock human potential that has always been there, waiting to be recognized, valued, and amplified. The question is not whether our children are capable. Rather, it is whether our institutions are ready to see and support the brilliance they bring.

"Culture is like wealth; it makes us more ourselves; it enables us to express ourselves." – Philip Gilbert Hamerton

CHAPTER FOUR: SPIRITUAL FOUNDATIONS OF LEARNING

"Just as love is a verb, so is faith." – **Nannie Helen Burroughs**

The test scores had come back, and they weren't good. Fifteen-year-old Malik sat at the kitchen table, his head in his hands, the weight of disappointing numbers pressing down on his shoulders like a heavy blanket. His mother, Sister Williams, poured herself a cup of coffee and sat across from him, her weathered hands folded in prayer position. Eventually, she broke her silence: "Baby," she said quietly, "let me tell you something my grandmother told me when I was about your age and struggling with my studies." She reached across the table and lifted his chin until their eyes met. "She said, 'Child, your worth ain't in no number on no paper. Your worth is in your spirit, and your spirit is connected to something bigger than any test could ever measure.'" She opened her worn Bible and turned to a passage she'd marked years ago. "It says right here in Jeremiah 29:11: 'For I know the plans I have for you, plans to prosper you and not to harm you, to give you hope and a future.' That test score? That's just information, baby. But your future? That's already written in love." Over the next hour, Malik's mother didn't dismiss the importance of academic achievement, but she placed it within a larger spiritual context that transformed failure from a verdict into a lesson, disappointment from an ending into a beginning. She helped him understand that his intelligence was a gift from the Divine, that his struggles were opportunities for growth, and that his education was part of a larger purpose that extended far beyond personal success.

This scene, repeated in countless Black homes across generations, illustrates a profound truth often overlooked in educational discussions: the spiritual dimensions of learning run deep in Black communities

(Ginwright, 2018; Nasir et al., 2020), providing foundations of hope, resilience, and purpose that sustain students through academic challenges and transform education from mere information transfer into soul development.

Faith, Hope, and Educational Transformation

In Black families, faith and education have always been intertwined (Clemons & Johnson, 2019; Clemons, 2024; Jeynes, 2016; Lincoln & Mamiya, 1990), not as separate domains but as complementary forces working toward human liberation and community uplift. This kind of integration creates a unique approach to learning that sees academic achievement as both a practical necessity and a spiritual calling.

Faith as Educational Foundation

The faith tradition in Black communities provides several crucial elements for educational success. First, it establishes the fundamental belief that every child is created with a divine purpose and unlimited potential. This isn't abstract theology—it's practical psychology that shapes how families approach their children's capabilities and challenges. When a grandmother looks at her struggling grandson and declares, "God don't make no mistakes, and He put greatness in you," she is doing more than merely offering comfort: she is establishing an unshakeable foundation of self-worth that transcends temporary academic difficulties.

This faith-based affirmation builds resilience, helping students persist through setbacks that might otherwise derail their educational journeys. The faith tradition also provides a framework for understanding struggle as purposeful rather than punitive. Students raised with spiritual foundations learn to see academic challenges not as evidence of inadequacy but as opportunities for growth, character development, and the strengthening of persistence, a very powerful perspective that transforms how they approach difficult subjects, failed tests, and learning obstacles.

Hope as Academic Fuel

Hope, in the Black spiritual tradition, is more than passive wishful thinking. It, instead, transcends into active expectation grounded in faith and demonstrated through works. This kind of hope becomes powerful fuel for educational achievement because it provides both vision and motivation for sustained effort: The parent who works multiple jobs while attending night school embodies hope in action, showing children that current circumstances don't define future possibilities; and the family that saves pennies for college funds despite financial struggles demonstrates hope made manifest through sacrifice and planning. These examples teach children that hope requires both faith and action, both vision and work.

This active hope also protects against the discouragement that can arise from systemic barriers and discrimination. When students understand their education as part of a larger spiritual journey toward purpose and service, temporary setbacks become stepping stones rather than stumbling blocks. They learn to see obstacles as tests of character rather than verdicts on capability.

Spiritual Community as Support System

The Black church and spiritual community have historically served as educational support systems, providing encouragement, resources, and accountability for students and families (Clemons & Johnson, 2019; Parker, 2021). This spiritual community model offers several crucial elements often missing from secular educational approaches. First, the church that celebrates academic achievements alongside spiritual milestones sends powerful messages about the connection between intellectual and spiritual growth (Clemons, 2024). The congregation that prays for students during exam periods provides emotional support that reduces anxiety and builds confidence. The spiritual mentor who connects biblical wisdom to academic challenges helps students see learning as part of their spiritual development. Secondly, these spiritual communities also provide alternative models of success and intelligence that can sustain students when traditional academic measures don't reflect their full capabilities. The Sunday school teacher who recognizes a student's wisdom and insight, the church musician who develops a teenager's mathematical understanding through rhythm and harmony, the deacon who mentors young people in leadership skills—these spiritual educators often see and develop talents that formal schooling misses.

Emotional Healing in Learning Environments

Education, particularly for Black students, often involves healing from various forms of trauma—historical trauma passed down through generations, personal trauma from discrimination and marginalization, and academic trauma from previous negative educational experiences (Ginwright, 2015). The spiritual foundations in Black communities provide unique resources for this healing work.

Sacred Space Creation. In many Black spiritual traditions, learning spaces are understood as sacred spaces where healing can occur alongside intellectual growth. This perspective transforms classrooms from mere information delivery systems into sanctuaries where students can experience restoration, affirmation, and transformation. The teacher who begins each day with a moment of centering is an effective educator who speaks life into students through affirmation, who creates classroom environments that feel like spiritual sanctuaries rather than academic battlegrounds. This great educator understands that healing often must precede learning. Students who have been wounded by previous educational experiences need to feel safe and affirmed before they can fully engage in academic risk-taking. This sacred space approach also recognizes that students bring their whole selves—including their pain, fears, and emotional baggage—into learning environments. Rather than ignoring these realities or demanding that students leave them at the door, spiritually grounded education acknowledges and addresses them as part of the learning process.

Forgiveness and Fresh Starts. The spiritual tradition of forgiveness provides powerful tools for academic healing and growth (Howard, 2019). Students who have experienced academic failure, who have been labeled as "problems" or "behind," who carry shame about their educational struggle, need the kind of fresh start that spiritual forgiveness offers. The educator who helps students forgive themselves for past academic failures creates space for new learning. The family that models grace in response to disappointing report cards while maintaining high expectations demonstrates how forgiveness and accountability can coexist. The students who learn to forgive teachers who may have underestimated them free themselves from resentment that could hinder future learning relationships. This work of forgiveness also extends to healing relationships between families and schools. Many Black families carry wounds from their own negative educational experiences or from watching their children struggle in unsupportive environments. Spiritual frameworks for forgiveness can help heal these wounds and create space for new partnerships focused on student success.

Prayer and Meditation as Learning Tools. While respecting the separation of church and state in public education, the spiritual practices of prayer and meditation offer powerful tools for learning enhancement that can be adapted for diverse educational settings. The quiet centering, for example, which begins with "Dear God, help me understand this math problem," can become the mindful focus that approaches complex problems with clarity and patience. The practice of gratitude that counts blessings can become the positive mindset that sees learning opportunities rather than obstacles. The meditation that seeks divine guidance can become a reflective practice that deepens understanding and insight. These spiritual practices teach students to access inner resources for learning—patience, persistence, faith in their own capabilities, and trust in the learning process. They provide alternatives to anxiety, frustration, and giving up when academic challenges arise.

Community Prayer and Support. The tradition of communal prayer and support in Black spiritual communities creates powerful networks of encouragement for educational achievement: When entire congregations commit to praying for students during exam periods, when families gather to pray over college applications, and when communities celebrate academic achievements as spiritual victories, these practices create emotional and spiritual support systems that sustain students through educational challenges. This communal support also helps students understand their individual educational success as part of community uplift and spiritual calling. They learn that their learning serves purposes larger than personal advancement—it honors the sacrifices of ancestors, fulfills divine purpose, and creates opportunities to serve others.

Connecting Spirit to Intellectual Growth

The artificial separation between spiritual development and intellectual growth represents a profound misunderstanding of how learning actually occurs in Black communities. The most effective educational approaches recognize and build upon the natural connections between spirit and intellect (Milner, 2020).

Wisdom vs. Knowledge. Black spiritual traditions distinguish between knowledge (information) and wisdom (understanding applied with moral and spiritual insight). This distinction provides crucial frameworks for education that go beyond mere information transfer to character development and life preparation. This wisdom-focused approach to education helps students see learning as personally meaningful rather than abstractly academic. When they understand how their studies connect to life purpose, community service, and spiritual development, they engage more deeply and persistently with challenging material. Thus, the student who memorizes historical facts demonstrates knowledge, but the student who understands how those historical patterns connect to current realities and future possibilities demonstrates wisdom. The child who can solve mathematical equations shows knowledge, but the young person who uses mathematical thinking to understand budgeting, planning, and resource allocation demonstrates wisdom.

Purpose-Driven Learning. Spiritual foundations provide students with a sense of purpose that transforms their relationship with education. Instead of learning for external rewards (grades, diplomas, parental approval), they learn because they understand their education as part of their spiritual calling and community responsibility. The teenager who studies medicine because they feel called to heal understands their struggles with organic chemistry as part of spiritual preparation for service. The young person who pursues education to teach children in their community sees their own learning challenges as preparation for understanding students' needs. This purpose-driven motivation sustains effort through difficulties that might otherwise lead to giving up. Moreover, purpose-driven learning also helps students maintain perspective during setbacks. When they understand their education as part of a larger spiritual journey, temporary failures become learning experiences rather than identity-defining verdicts. They develop the long-term perspective that sees growth over time rather than demanding immediate perfection.

Stewardship of Gifts. The spiritual concept of stewardship—the idea that our talents and abilities are gifts to be developed and used for service—provides a powerful framework for academic motivation and responsibility. Students who understand their intelligence as a divine gift to be stewarded or shared approach learning with a different attitude than those who see it as personal possession to be hoarded. This stewardship perspective also creates internal motivation for academic excellence, as students understand that failing to develop their capabilities represents poor stewardship of divine gifts. It also motivates them to use their education in service to others, as they view their learning as preparation for community contribution rather than just personal advancement. The stewardship framework likewise provides a healthy perspective on both success and failure. Success becomes an opportunity for gratitude and increased responsibility rather than a basis for pride or superiority. Failure becomes a call for better stewardship rather than evidence of unworthiness or inability.

Integration of Heart and Mind. Black spiritual traditions resist the false dichotomy between emotional/spiritual development and intellectual growth, for they understand that the most profound learning engages both heart and mind, both feeling and thinking, both soul and intellect (Nasir et al., 2020). For example, the Sunday school lesson that uses biblical stories to teach moral reasoning develops both spiritual insight and critical thinking skills, the gospel song that requires mathematical understanding of rhythm and harmony integrates artistic expression with analytical thinking, and the community service project that applies academic knowledge to real-world problems connects intellectual learning with spiritual calling all provide poignant examples of the integration of the heart and mind dynamic. This integrated approach further recognizes that students are whole human beings who learn best when all dimensions of their humanity are engaged and valued. It creates educational experiences that are emotionally satisfying, intellectually challenging, and spiritually meaningful.

Practical Applications for Educators and Families

Understanding the spiritual foundations of learning in Black communities provides practical guidance for educators and families seeking to support student success.

Creating Spiritually Responsive Learning Environments. While respecting religious diversity and the separation of church and state, educators can create learning environments that honor the spiritual dimensions of students' lives. These might include moments of reflection and centering, opportunities for students to connect learning to their values and purposes, and recognition of students' spiritual resources for resilience and motivation.

Holistic Approach to Student Support. Support services that address students' spiritual and emotional needs alongside academic challenges often prove more effective than purely academic interventions. These services might include counseling that helps students process academic trauma, mentoring that connects learning to life purpose, and family engagement that honors spiritual values.

Purpose-Centered Curriculum. Educational approaches that help students connect their learning to larger purposes and calling create deeper engagement and motivation. Approaches of this kind might include service-learning projects, career exploration that considers calling alongside earning potential, and academic content that connects to students' spiritual and community values.

Strengths-Based Assessment. Strengths-based assessment is a practical approach that uses evaluation methods that recognize spiritual resources such as resilience, hope, and purpose, alongside traditional academic measures, to provide a more complete picture of students' capabilities and potential (Milner, 2020).

The Transformative Power of Spiritual Integration

When educational approaches recognize and build upon the spiritual foundations that Black students bring to learning, transformation occurs at multiple levels (Ginwright, 2018; Parker et al., 2025). Students develop deeper engagement with academic content because they understand its connection to their spiritual development and life purpose. They demonstrate greater resilience in facing academic challenges because they have spiritual resources for persistence and hope, and they show increased motivation for academic excellence because they understand their learning as stewardship of divine gifts and preparation for community service. Families experience stronger partnerships with schools when their spiritual values are respected and integrated rather than ignored or dismissed. Communities see greater educational success when schools recognize and build upon the spiritual capital that families bring to education.

The integration of spiritual foundations with intellectual development does not diminish academic rigor, but it enhances it by providing motivation, resilience, and purpose that sustain students through the demanding work of learning. Moreover, it creates educational experiences that honor students' full humanity and prepare them not just for career success but for lives of meaning, service, and contribution.

The spiritual foundations of learning in Black communities then offer profound wisdom for educational transformation. They remind us that true education involves not just the development of intellectual capabilities but the nurturing of spiritual resources that sustain learners through challenges and connect their learning to purposes larger than themselves. When we honor these spiritual foundations, we create educational experiences that transform not just minds but hearts, not just individuals but communities, not just present circumstances but future possibilities.

"You are the source of my strength. You are the strength of my life. I lift my hands in total praise to You." – **Richard Smallwood**

CHAPTER FIVE: NEURODIVERSITY IN BLACK FAMILIES

"We all have different gifts, so we all have different ways of saying to the world who we are." - **Fred Rogers**

Eight-year-old Zara couldn't sit still during story time. While other children sat cross-legged on the carpet, she paced the perimeter of the reading circle, her fingers tracing patterns in the air as she absorbed every word of the tale. Her teacher saw disruption—a child who couldn't follow simple instructions, who distracted others, who needed to be "fixed."

Her grandmother saw something different entirely: "That child got the spirit moving through her," Grandma Pearl would say, watching Zara dance through math problems, literally jumping from one solution to another. "She think with her whole body, not just her head. Ain't nothing wrong with that—that's how God made her brain work." When the school suggested testing for ADHD and possible medication, Grandma Pearl didn't dismiss the idea entirely, but she insisted on a different conversation first. She shared stories of Uncle Jerome, who couldn't read traditional books but could take apart and rebuild any engine by the time he was twelve. She talked about Cousin Denise, whose "spaciness" in school became innovative thinking in her engineering career. She reminded the family that different didn't mean deficient.

"We been having all kinds of minds in our family forever," she told Zara's parents. "Some folks think in straight lines, some think in circles, some think in colors and music and movement. The world needs all kinds of thinking. Our job is to help Zara use her kind of thinking to do great things." This wisdom, born from generations of nurturing diverse minds within Black families, challenges the deficit-based models that too often pathologize neurodivergent learners, particularly Black children who face the double burden of racial bias and ableism in educational settings (Annamma, 2017; Annamma et al, 2018; Coker et al, 2016; Connor et al., 2021; DeMatthews, 2020; Dwyer, 2022; Fadus et al., 2020).

Celebrating Different Learning Approaches

Black families have long understood that intelligence manifests in countless ways, that learning occurs through multiple pathways, and that what the dominant culture labels as "disorders" may instead be different ways of engaging with the world that carry their own gifts and strengths.

The Rhythm Learner. In many Black families, children who struggle with traditional sit-still-and-listen learning styles are recognized as rhythm learners—students who process information through movement, music, and kinesthetic engagement. Rather than forcing these children into restrictive learning boxes, families often find ways to honor their need for movement while supporting their academic growth. Children who memorize multiplication tables by turning them into rap songs are not avoiding real learning; rather, they are accessing it through their natural processing style. Students who need to keep pace while reading are not being disruptive; they are instead regulating their nervous systems to maintain focus (Waitoller & Thorius, 2016). Likewise, teenagers who doodle during lectures are not being disrespectful. On the contrary, they use visual processing to support auditory learning.

These rhythm learners often possess exceptional abilities in areas that traditional education undervalues: they excel in creative problem-solving, demonstrate remarkable spatial intelligence, show advanced understanding of patterns and systems, and often possess heightened empathy and emotional intelligence (Waitoller & Thorius, 2016; Leadbitter et al., 2021).

The Deep Dive Thinker. Some neurodivergent learners in Black families are recognized as deep dive thinkers—students who may struggle with surface-level interactions but demonstrate extraordinary depth and focus when pursuing their interests. These children might seem "obsessed" with particular topics, but families often understand this intensity as a gift rather than a problem.

The child, therefore, who can tell you everything about trains but struggles with small talk, possesses systematic thinking that could lead to engineering excellence. The teenager who memorizes every detail of their favorite historical period but appears disorganized in other subjects demonstrates the kind of passionate expertise that drives innovation and discovery. The young person who creates elaborate fantasy worlds but struggles with basic social interactions shows creative intelligence that could transform storytelling, game design, or therapeutic practices.

The Quiet Observer. In cultures that often value verbal expression and social interaction, quiet, introverted learners can be misunderstood or overlooked. But many Black families recognize the wisdom of the quiet observer—the child who processes internally, who notices details others miss, who thinks deeply before speaking. These learners often demonstrate exceptional analytical abilities, creative insights, and deep empathy. They might struggle in group discussions but excel in written expression. They might seem withdrawn in large gatherings but show remarkable depth in one-on-one interactions. They might appear not to be paying attention, but often absorb and retain information more effectively than their more vocal peers.

The Sensory Navigator. Black children with sensory processing differences—those who are hypersensitive to sounds, textures, lights, or who seek intense sensory input—are often understood in Black families as sensory navigators who experience the world more intensely than others. Children who cover their ears during fire drills are not being dramatic, but they are managing sensory overload that feels genuinely painful. Students who need to touch everything to understand it are not being disruptive; they are just using their tactile processing system to make sense of abstract concepts. Finally, teenagers who seem overwhelmed by crowded hallways are not being antisocial; they are instead protecting themselves from sensory input that could derail their ability to learn.

Supporting and Empowering Neurodivergent Learners

Black families have developed sophisticated strategies for supporting neurodivergent learners, often without formal diagnoses or professional interventions. These grassroots approaches, refined through generations of loving different kinds of minds, offer valuable insights for both families and educators.

Creating Home Learning Sanctuaries. Many Black families instinctively understand that neurodivergent learners need spaces designed around their particular needs rather than fighting against their natural tendencies. This might mean creating quiet corners for deep thinkers, movement zones for kinesthetic learners, or sensory-friendly spaces for children who need careful environmental management. The grandmother who allows her ADHD grandson to stand at the kitchen counter to do homework while she cooks recognizes that movement and familiar background activity might help his focus rather than hinder it. The parent who creates a cozy reading nook with soft lighting and weighted blankets for their anxious child recognizes that emotional regulation supports cognitive function. The family that designates certain times as "quiet hours" for their introverted learner demonstrates an understanding that different minds require different conditions to thrive.

Strengths-Based Advocacy. Rather than focusing primarily on deficits and challenges, many Black families become fierce advocates for their neurodivergent children by highlighting their strengths and capabilities. This strengths-based advocacy is often more effective than deficit-focused approaches in securing appropriate educational support. The parent who documents their child's exceptional memory for historical details and notes their struggles with organization presents a complete picture that helps educators understand how to build on strengths while addressing challenges. The family that shares examples of their child's creative problem-solving abilities, along with requests for academic accommodations, provides context that transforms educators' perceptions of the student.

Cultural Code-Switching Support. Neurodivergent Black children often face the additional challenge of learning to navigate between their authentic selves and societal expectations while also managing their neurological differences. Families often provide crucial support in developing these code-switching skills without losing authenticity. This might mean teaching children when and how to use stimming behaviors that help them self-regulate without drawing negative attention. It could involve helping teenagers understand how to advocate for their needs in academic settings while maintaining dignity and respect. It often includes conversations about how neurological differences intersect with racial identity and the importance of finding communities that accept and celebrate both.

Intergenerational Wisdom Sharing. In many Black families, older generations share stories and strategies that help normalize neurodivergent experiences and provide practical guidance for success. These stories often reveal that neurodiversity has always existed in families, even when it wasn't formally recognized or labeled. The grandfather who struggled with reading but became a successful craftsman provides evidence that academic challenges don't define life potential. The aunt who was always "different" but found her place as a gifted artist exemplifies how neurodivergent traits can become professional strengths. The older cousin who found success in a non-traditional career path shows that there are many routes to achievement and fulfillment, all of which exemplify intergenerational wisdom sharing.

Challenging Deficit Models of Learning Differences

The dominant educational and medical models often approach neurodivergence through deficit-based thinking—focusing on what students cannot do, what's "wrong" with their brains, and how they need to be "fixed" to fit into existing systems. Black families, drawing on cultural wisdom about human diversity and systemic critique, often challenge these deficit models in powerful ways.

Reframing "Symptoms" as Characteristics. Where medical models see symptoms to be treated, many Black families see characteristics to be understood and supported. This reframing fundamentally changes how children understand themselves and their neurological differences. The child whose "hyperactivity" is reframed as "high energy that needs positive outlets" develops a different relationship with their movement needs. The student whose "attention deficit" is understood as "attention that works differently and needs different supports" maintains dignity while receiving help. The teenager whose "social difficulties" are seen as "different social preferences that deserve respect" avoids the shame often associated with autism diagnoses. Reframing symptoms as characteristics does not mean denying the real challenges that neurodivergent individuals face; rather, it approaches those challenges from a position of strength and acceptance, rather than pathology and deficit.

Questioning Cultural Biases in Assessment. Black families often bring healthy skepticism to assessment processes, recognizing that cultural biases can influence how neurodivergent traits are interpreted, particularly in Black children who may face racial stereotypes alongside ableist assumptions. Accordingly, the behavior that's seen as "aggressive" or "defiant" in a Black child with ADHD might be interpreted as "energetic" or "spirited" in a white child with the same condition (Coker, et al, 2016; Shi et al, 2021). Likewise, the social communication differences that lead to autism diagnoses in middle-class white families might be misunderstood as "behavioral problems" in Black children from different cultural backgrounds (Aylward et al, 2021; Habayeb et al, 2021; Pham et al, 2022). Families who understand these biases often advocate for culturally competent assessment and support services that recognize how race and disability intersect to create unique experiences and needs.

Celebrating Neurodivergent Contributions. Rather than seeing neurodivergence as something to overcome, many Black families celebrate the unique contributions that different kinds of minds bring to families and communities. This celebration helps neurodivergent children develop a positive sense of identity and self-worth. The family that recognizes their ADHD child's ability to think outside the box and come up with creative solutions helps that child see their difference as a gift. The community that values its autistic members' attention to detail and systematic thinking shows how neurodivergent traits contribute to collective success. The extended family that appreciates their dyslexic relative's storytelling abilities and spatial intelligence demonstrates how different kinds of intelligence serve different purposes.

Intergenerational Strategies for Neurodivergent Success

Black families often develop and pass down sophisticated strategies to support the success of neurodivergent individuals across generations. These intergenerational approaches recognize that supporting neurodivergent learners is a long-term, community-wide endeavor that benefits from accumulated wisdom and shared responsibility.

The Wisdom Keeper Tradition. In many families, certain members become wisdom keepers who specialize in understanding and supporting neurodivergent relatives. These wisdom keepers might be grandparents who've raised multiple generations of learners, aunts who work in education or healthcare, or older siblings who've navigated similar challenges successfully. These wisdom keepers serve multiple functions: they provide practical strategies based on experience, offer emotional support and advocacy, help interpret professional recommendations in culturally relevant ways, and maintain family stories that normalize neurodivergent experiences.

The Success Story Archive. Families often maintain formal or informal archives of success stories that provide hope and guidance for younger neurodivergent members. These stories serve as evidence that challenges can be overcome, that different paths to success exist, and that neurodivergent traits can become professional and personal strengths, as the following examples illustrate:

The uncle who couldn't sit still in school but became a successful entrepreneur shows ADHD children that their energy can be channeled into achievement; the cousin who struggled with traditional academics but excelled in culinary arts demonstrates that intelligence comes in many forms; and the neighbor who found success in a field that values their particular kind of thinking provides a concrete model of how neurodivergent traits can become career assets.

The Network Expansion Strategy. Successful support for neurodivergent learners often requires expanding beyond immediate family to include chosen family, community members, and professional allies who understand and support diverse minds. Intergenerational wisdom includes knowing how to build these networks effectively. Utilizing this wisdom involves connecting with other families who have neurodivergent children, finding educators who embrace neurodiversity, identifying healthcare providers who take a strengths-based approach, or locating community programs that celebrate different kinds of intelligence.

The Long-Term Perspective. Intergenerational approaches to supporting neurodivergent learners emphasize long-term development over short-term fixes. This perspective helps families avoid panic responses to temporary setbacks and maintain faith in their children's ultimate potential. The grandmother, for example, who reminds parents that their struggling eight-year-old has decades to develop their gifts provides crucial perspective during difficult periods. The family that focuses on character development and life skills alongside academic achievement prepares neurodivergent children for long-term success rather than just immediate compliance.

Twice-Exceptional Black Students: Brilliance and Barriers

Within Black families and communities, neurodiversity often appears not as a problem to be solved but as a complexity to be understood. One especially misunderstood group is twice-exceptional—or *2E*—students: children who demonstrate advanced intellectual ability while also living with learning disabilities or other forms of neurodivergence (Annamma et al., 2018; Clemons & Mayes, 2024). These learners may be exceptional in abstract reasoning, verbal expression, or strategic thinking while simultaneously struggling with attention regulation, sensory processing, reading comprehension, or executive functioning.

Twice-exceptionality disrupts narrow definitions of giftedness. A child may read years above grade level yet experience emotional overwhelm in loud classrooms. Another may excel in logic-based games and spatial reasoning, while finding routine tasks or sequential directions exhausting. In many school systems, such contradictions confuse educators accustomed to equating giftedness with uniform academic performance. As a result, the child's disability often dominates the narrative while their brilliance remains hidden—or their gifts mask the support they desperately need (Connor et al., 2021).

Why 2E Black Students Are Missed

Black twice-exceptional students encounter layered barriers that compound the already difficult process of identification. Racial bias in gifted education, culturally narrow testing practices, and deficit-oriented interpretations of behavior frequently prevent educators from recognizing both sides of a child's profile (Annamma et al, 2018; Clemons & Cokley, 2022; Fadus et al., 2019; Hatton & Clemons, 2022). Intersectionality—the navigation of racial, academic, and neurodivergent identities at once (Crenshaw, 1989)—shapes how these students experience school, often intensifying stereotype threat and pressure to conform.

When schools focus primarily on perceived deficits, children internalize messages that something is wrong with them rather than understanding their minds as complex and powerful. Social-emotional strain, masking behaviors, and withdrawal may follow as students attempt to fit into systems that fail to recognize their full humanity (Leadbitter et al., 2021).

Reframing Identification Through Strength. Black families frequently resist these narrow frames by centering brilliance first and challenge second. Identification strategies rooted in equity emphasize collaboration among families, counselors, teachers, and community members; multiple measures of ability; flexible eligibility criteria; and recognition of culturally mediated expressions of giftedness (Waitoller & Thorius, 2016; Clemons, 2024).

Broadening definitions of excellence—so that storytelling, leadership, creativity, movement, and relational intelligence count as markers of giftedness—allows twice-exceptional Black learners to be seen in their fullness rather than filtered through narrow assessment lenses.

Community-Centered Support and Advocacy. Effective intervention requires culturally responsive counseling, strong family partnerships, flexible learning environments, mentorship programs, and proactive advocacy for IEPs or 504 plans. Group spaces where students can process experiences of marginalization alongside intellectual challenge help restore confidence and belonging, while mentorship connects children to adults who model thriving twice-exceptional futures (Connor et al., 2021).

Black communities have long practiced this kind of holistic care—drawing on extended kin networks, educators, faith institutions, and local leaders to nurture children's talents while buffering them from harm. For twice-exceptional learners, such village-based systems become essential counterweights to deficit narratives and powerful engines of possibility.

Reframing Disability as a Form of Cultural Strength

Perhaps the most radical contribution of Black family wisdom to understanding neurodiversity is reframing disability from individual deficit to cultural strength—the recognition that different kinds of minds contribute essential perspectives and abilities that strengthen communities and advance human knowledge.

The Innovation Perspective. Many Black families understand that the same neurodivergent traits that create challenges in traditional educational settings often drive innovation, creativity, and breakthrough thinking in professional and creative endeavors. This perspective helps neurodivergent children see their differences as potential superpowers rather than just obstacles to overcome. Thus, the hyperfocus that makes ADHD children struggle with transitions can become the intense concentration that drives scientific discovery. The pattern recognition that characterizes many autistic minds can lead to breakthroughs in technology, mathematics, and system design. The creative thinking that makes dyslexic students struggle with traditional reading can become the innovative problem-solving that transforms industries.

The Community Contribution Model. Rather than seeing neurodivergent individuals as burdens to be supported, many Black families operate from community contribution models that recognize how different kinds of minds serve different community functions and needs: The detail-oriented autistic family member who, for example, notices when community systems aren't working properly serves as a quality control specialist for family and neighborhood decisions; The ADHD teenager whose high energy and enthusiasm motivates others becomes a natural leader and encourager; the anxious child whose sensitivity to social dynamics helps prevent conflicts becomes a valuable mediator and relationship counselor.

The Survival Wisdom Framework. Some Black families view neurodivergent traits as survival wisdom—neurological adaptations that helped ancestors navigate dangerous, unpredictable environments and that continue to provide valuable capabilities in modern contexts. The hypervigilance that characterizes some anxiety and ADHD presentations can be understood as survival awareness that helped ancestors detect danger and respond quickly to threats. The systematic thinking that characterizes autism can be seen as a cognitive organization that helped communities manage complex resource allocation and social relationships. The sensory sensitivity that creates challenges in modern environments might have also provided crucial environmental awareness in ancestral contexts.

The Resistance Intelligence Perspective. Some neurodivergent traits can be understood as forms of resistance intelligence—neurological patterns that resist conformity, challenge assumptions, and refuse to accept inadequate systems and explanations. Consider these examples: The ADHD child who questions everything and refuses to accept "because I said so" as an answer demonstrates critical thinking that could drive social change; the autistic teenager who insists on logical consistency and fairness shows moral reasoning that could transform unjust systems; and the dyslexic student who finds creative workarounds for reading challenges demonstrates the kind of innovative thinking that bypasses barriers and creates new possibilities.

Practical Applications

Understanding neurodiversity through the lens of Black family wisdom provides practical guidance for families, educators, and communities seeking to support neurodivergent learners effectively.

Culturally Responsive Assessment and Support. Assessment and intervention approaches must recognize how cultural background influences the expression and interpretation of neurodivergent traits. These approaches include understanding how racial bias affects diagnostic processes, how cultural communication styles might be misinterpreted as social deficits, and how traditional professional models might not recognize family strengths and resources.

Strength-Based Educational Planning. Educational approaches that build on neurodivergent students' strengths and interests while providing support for challenging areas often prove more effective than deficit-focused remediation. Approaches of this kind might include project-based learning that allows for different kinds of expression, flexible seating and movement options, or curriculum modifications that connect to students' passionate interests, showing the efficacy of strength-based educational planning.

Family Partnership Models. Schools and support services that recognize families as experts on their neurodivergent children and that build on family wisdom and strategies often achieve better outcomes than approaches that dismiss or undervalue family knowledge and experience.

Community Building and Peer Support. Creating communities where neurodivergent individuals and their families can connect, share strategies, and celebrate successes helps combat isolation and builds collective wisdom about supporting different kinds of minds.

The Transformation Imperative

Embracing neurodiversity as a cultural strength rather than an individual deficit has the potential to transform not just how we support neurodivergent learners, but also how we think about human diversity, educational effectiveness, and community building more broadly. When we recognize that different kinds of minds contribute essential perspectives and abilities, we create educational systems that honor all learners rather than forcing conformity to narrow definitions of "normal." When we view neurodivergent traits as potential strengths rather than just challenges to overcome, we help all students build more positive relationships with their unique capabilities and learning styles.

Ultimately, we must understand and wisely accept that the wisdom that Black families bring to supporting neurodivergent learners—the understanding that all minds have value, that different doesn't mean deficient, that community support can help individuals thrive, and that diversity strengthens rather than weakens communities—offers crucial guidance for creating more inclusive and effective educational approaches.

The neurodivergent learners in our families and communities are not broken systems in need of repair—they are different kinds of minds that bring essential perspectives, innovative thinking, and unique contributions to our collective human experience. When we learn to see and support these gifts, we create educational environments where all learners can thrive, where diversity is celebrated rather than merely tolerated, and where different ways of thinking and learning are recognized as sources of strength rather than obstacles to overcome.

The operative question is not how to make neurodivergent learners fit into existing systems, but how to create systems that are flexible and wise enough to support the full spectrum of human neurodiversity. Black families have been answering this question for generations, believing that different abilities still mean possibilities. Now is the time for educational institutions to learn from their wisdom.

"Allow me to learn in a way that's best for me and watch me outperform the masses." – Special Ed Resource

CHAPTER SIX: RESISTANCE AND LIBERATION THROUGH EDUCATION

"Education is the most powerful weapon which you can use to change the world." - **Nelson Mandela**

Mama Ruth used to tell her grandchildren that every time they opened a book, they opened a door that nobody could ever close again. She understood what generations of Black families have known: that education is not just about acquiring knowledge; it is about claiming power, challenging systems, and creating new possibilities where none existed before.

In the sacred space between home and school, between what is and what could be, Black families have always understood education as an act of resistance (Anderson, 1988; Freire, 2020; Engram Jr., 2023). This understanding runs deeper than test scores or graduation rates. It reaches into the very heart of what it means to transform not just individual lives, but entire communities and systems that have historically sought to limit our children's potential.

Learning as an Act of Empowerment

When twelve-year-old Marcus walks into his seventh-grade classroom carrying the weight of his grandmother's stories about segregated schools, he carries something more powerful than any textbook: the knowledge that his very presence in that classroom is a victory won through generations of struggle. His grandmother, Mrs. Williams, made sure he understood this legacy not as a burden, but as a source of strength. Poignantly, she would say, "Baby," she would say, adjusting his backpack each morning, "your great-great-grandmother couldn't read because it was against the law. Your great-grandmother learned to read by candlelight after working in the fields all day. Your grandmother integrated the high school in this town.

Every time you raise your hand in that classroom, you're continuing a revolution."

This story, one of hundreds, is the wisdom that Black families bring to education: the understanding that learning is inherently political, inherently transformative, and inherently connected to liberation (Freire, 2020; Ladson-Billings, 2021). When we frame education as empowerment, we move beyond the narrow confines of standardized metrics and into the realm of human possibility. Thus, the empowerment that comes through education manifests in multiple ways within Black family traditions. There's the intellectual empowerment that comes from critical thinking and questioning systems. There's the cultural empowerment that comes from understanding one's history and heritage. There's the economic empowerment that comes from accessing opportunities previously denied. And there's the spiritual empowerment that comes from knowing you have the capacity to contribute meaningfully to your community's progress.

Additionally, consider the tradition of "kitchen table tutorials" that happens in countless Black homes across the country. Around kitchen tables, over homework and dinner preparations, parents and grandparents don't just help with math problems—they teach children to see connections between their studies and their lives, between their potential and their community's needs. These informal educational moments are sites of profound empowerment, where children learn that their education belongs to them and serves purposes far greater than individual advancement. The grandmother who helps her granddaughter with a science project while sharing stories of Black inventors teaches a powerful lesson: that brilliance and innovation have always existed in our communities, even when textbooks failed to acknowledge it. The father who connects his son's history assignment to family genealogy teaches that academic learning and family wisdom are not separate streams but part of the same flowing river of knowledge.

How Education Challenges Systemic Barriers

Black families have long understood that education is both shaped by systemic barriers that are nevertheless capable of challenging them. This dual reality requires a sophisticated approach to navigating educational systems while working to transform them.

These barriers are real and persistent: Under-resourced schools, biased curricula, discriminatory discipline policies, and lowered expectations create obstacles that can seem insurmountable. But within Black family wisdom lies a treasure trove of strategies for not just surviving these systems but actively working to change them. Take the example of the Johnson family, whose children attend a school where Black history is relegated to a single month of superficial coverage. Rather than accepting this limitation, the family creates what they call "365 Black History" at home. They weave stories of Black achievement, struggle, and triumph into daily conversations. They visit museums, attend cultural events, and connect with elders who lived through pivotal moments in civil rights history. When their children return to school, they carry with them a rich understanding of their heritage that no curriculum gap can diminish.

This family approach does more than fill educational voids: it challenges the very premise that schools are the sole authorities on what knowledge matters, and it asserts that families are legitimate sources of wisdom and that children deserve educational experiences that reflect the fullness of human experience and achievement. The systemic challenge of educating Black children extends beyond content to pedagogy itself. Black families thus often find themselves advocating for teaching approaches that recognize their children's learning styles, cultural backgrounds, and community experiences. Black families advocating for their kids possibly means pushing for more collaborative learning environments that mirror the communal values of many Black families; they must likewise be persistent in advocating for assessment methods that capture the full range of student abilities rather than relying solely on standardized tests.

In a very practical sense, consider the mother who notices her daughter's math grades improving dramatically when she frames word problems in contexts familiar to the child's experience. She doesn't just celebrate the improvement—she questions why the school's curriculum doesn't naturally include diverse contexts that speak to all students' experiences. She joins the parent-teacher organization, volunteers in the classroom, and gradually introduces ideas about culturally responsive teaching. Her individual advocacy becomes part of a larger movement toward more inclusive educational practice. Essentially, the power of this approach lies in its recognition that challenging systemic barriers requires both individual and collective action. Families prepare their children to navigate existing systems while simultaneously working to create better systems for all children. They teach their children to excel within current structures while maintaining a critical consciousness about those structures' limitations and potential for transformation.

Turning Classrooms into Spaces of Possibility

The transformation of classrooms into spaces of possibility requires a fundamental shift in how we understand the relationship between families, students, and schools. Black family wisdom offers a vision of classrooms as sites of liberation where every student's full humanity is recognized, celebrated, and nurtured. This transformation begins with the recognition that students bring assets, not deficits, into the classroom (Ladson-Billings, 2021; Paris & Alim, 2017). Examples of these assets include but are not limited to the child who translates for her grandmother, multilingual skills and cultural bridge-building abilities, the student who helps manage household finances while parents work multiple jobs, bringing mathematical reasoning and responsibility; and the young person who mediates conflicts in their neighborhood, bringing peacemaking and leadership skills. When classrooms become spaces that recognize and build upon these assets, they become sites of empowerment rather than remediation.

The concept of "funds of knowledge (González et al., 2005)"—the idea that all families possess wisdom and skills that can enhance educational experiences—becomes central to this transformation. A classroom becomes a space of possibility when the grandmother's knowledge of herbal remedies connects to the chemistry curriculum, when the father's experience as a mechanic enriches the physics lesson, and when the mother's community organizing skills inform the social studies discussion about civic engagement. Consider the third-grade classroom where Mrs. Thompson, inspired by conversations with Black families in her school community, transforms her teaching approach. Instead of starting the year with generic getting-to-know-you activities, she begins with a family heritage project that invites students to research and share their family histories. The classroom walls become galleries of family wisdom, featuring stories of migration, innovation, survival, and triumph. In the same way, when eight-year-old Destiny shares her great-grandfather's story of learning to read as an adult after being denied education as a child, the classroom engages in a rich discussion about the value of education and the courage required to pursue learning despite obstacles. When Jamal presents his grandmother's recipe for sweet potato pie alongside a mathematical exploration of fractions and measurements, the classroom discovers that learning can be both rigorous and culturally affirming. These classrooms become spaces where critical thinking flourishes because students are encouraged to question, analyze, and connect their learning to real-world experiences. They become spaces where creativity thrives because students see their own cultures and experiences reflected and valued. They become spaces where academic excellence is pursued not for its own sake, but as a tool for community transformation and personal empowerment.

The role of the teacher in these transformed spaces is not to be the sole source of knowledge, but to be a facilitator of learning that draws from multiple sources of wisdom (Gay, 2018; Sealey-Ruiz et al., 2021). Teachers become cultural brokers who help students navigate between home and school knowledge, who create bridges between academic content and community experience, who recognize that learning is most powerful when it connects to students' lives and dreams. The transformation extends beyond individual classrooms to encompass entire school cultures. Schools become spaces of possibility when they actively seek input from Black families, create multiple pathways for family engagement, and recognize that parent conferences and PTA meetings are just one way families can contribute to educational excellence (Ladson-Billings, 2021; Paris & Alim, 2017).

Picture the school that creates a "Community Wisdom Council" composed of elders from the surrounding neighborhood who share their experiences and knowledge with students. The retired teacher who offers after-school tutoring sessions that blend academic support with life lessons. The grandmother who teaches traditional crafts while incorporating lessons about geometry and history. The community activist who leads student discussions about social justice and civic engagement. These schools understand that the village that raises a child extends far beyond the school building. They actively cultivate partnerships with community organizations, faith institutions, and cultural centers. They recognize that some of the most powerful learning happens when students see connections between their classroom studies and their community's needs and aspirations.

The ultimate goal of turning classrooms into spaces of possibility is to prepare students not just for academic success, but for lives of purpose and impact. These spaces nurture what Paulo Freire called "critical consciousness (2020)"—the ability to read both the word and the world, to understand how knowledge connects to power, and to use education as a tool for both personal advancement and social transformation. In these transformed educational spaces, students learn that they are not just recipients of education but active creators of knowledge. They understand that their questions matter, their perspectives are valuable, and their dreams are achievable. They develop not just academic skills but also the confidence, creativity, and critical thinking abilities needed to address the challenges and opportunities they will face in life.

The Legacy Continues

The wisdom embedded in Black family approaches to education as resistance and liberation continues to evolve and adapt. Today's parents and grandparents build upon generations of educational activism while addressing contemporary challenges and opportunities. They also navigate digital learning environments while maintaining the emphasis on human connection and community that has always characterized Black educational traditions. The parent who advocates for more diverse literature in the classroom carries forward the tradition of the grandmother who supplemented inadequate textbooks with rich oral histories. The student who starts a Black Student Union at her school continues the legacy of young people who organized sit-ins and freedom rides (Engram Jr., 2023; Tatum, 2017). The teacher who implements culturally responsive pedagogy honors the wisdom of families who have always known that children learn best when their full selves are welcomed into the educational process.

This continuing legacy reminds us that education as resistance and liberation is not a historical artifact but a living, breathing approach to learning that evolves to meet each generation's challenges and opportunities. It calls us to see every classroom as a potential site of transformation, every student as a carrier of wisdom and possibility, and every family as a partner in the sacred work of education. The village that raises a classroom understands that true educational excellence emerges when we honor the full humanity of every student, when we create spaces where all voices are heard and valued, and when we use education not just to transmit knowledge but to transform communities and expand possibilities for all children (Freire, 2020; Engram Jr., 2023).

With this vision, resistance and liberation through education are not just about overcoming barriers: they are about creating new realities where all children can thrive, where all families are valued as educational partners, and where all communities benefit from the full development of their young people's potential. This is the gift that Black family wisdom offers to the broader educational community: a vision of learning that is both deeply rooted in community and expansively oriented toward liberation and possibility.

"My work is rooted in resistance because it was born from resistance." – **Dr. Frederick V. Engram**

CHAPTER SEVEN: NAVIGATING INSTITUTIONAL CHALLENGES

"I had to make my own living and my own opportunity. But I made it! Don't sit down and wait for the opportunities to come. Get up and make them." - **Madam C.J. Walker**

Sister Margaret knew the drill by heart. Every September, as she prepared her grandson Terrell for another school year, she would sit him down for what the family called "The Talk"—not just about the birds and the bees, but about surviving and thriving in spaces that weren't always designed for children like him. Her weathered hands would smooth his shirt collar as she spoke words that had been passed down through generations: "Baby, you're twice as good, but you're gonna have to be three times as prepared." This ritual—repeated in countless Black households across the nation and powerfully dramatized in the television series *Scandal*—represents far more than parental caution; it reflects a sophisticated strategy for surviving and navigating institutions while preserving dignity, purpose, and hope (Carter Andrews et al., 2019). It reflects the accumulated wisdom of families who have learned to transform obstacles into opportunities, discrimination into determination, and systemic barriers into stepping stones toward excellence.

For generations, Black families have understood—often through painful experience—that educational institutions can simultaneously promise opportunity and reproduce harm. Contemporary scholarship shows that anti-Blackness in schooling does not operate only through overt acts of racism; it is sustained through lowered academic expectations, disproportionate discipline, surveillance, curricular marginalization, and tracking practices that position Black children as risks rather than as learners worthy of care and intellectual challenge (Dumas, 2016; Love, 2019). These patterns explain why "The Talk" emerges in households like Sister Margaret's—not as cynicism, but as a strategy. Families teach children to document interactions, advocate assertively, code-switch when necessary, and perform excellence because they recognize how racialized systems can distort perception (Kendi, 2016; Yosso, 2005). Such preparation reflects sophisticated institutional literacy: a collective knowledge base developed to help children survive and thrive in environments where fairness cannot always be assumed but dignity must always be protected.

Strategies for Surviving and Thriving

The difference between surviving and thriving in challenging institutional environments lies not only in individual resilience but also in the collective strategies that Black families have developed and refined over generations. These strategies operate on multiple levels simultaneously: preparing children psychologically for challenges they may face (Stevenson, 2014; Neblett et al., 2016), equipping them with practical tools for success, and building networks of support that extend far beyond the nuclear family.

Consider the approach taken by the Harrison family when their daughter, Jasmine, enrolled at a prestigious preparatory school where she was one of only a handful of Black students. Rather than simply hoping for the best, they developed what they called their "Excellence Blueprint"—a comprehensive strategy that addressed academic preparation, social navigation, and emotional wellness:

The Academic Component. The academic component involved not only ensuring that Jasmine was prepared for rigorous coursework but also teaching her to advocate for herself in classroom discussions, to seek help when needed without shame, and to recognize that her presence in advanced classes was not an accident but the result of her abilities and preparation. Her parents connected her with older students who had navigated similar environments, creating an informal mentorship network that provided both practical advice and emotional support.

Social Navigation Strategy. The social navigation aspect recognized that academic success occurs within a complex web of relationships and unwritten rules. Jasmine learned to read social cues, to build authentic friendships across racial lines while maintaining connections to her cultural community, and to handle both microaggressions and overt racism with grace and strength. Her family helped her understand that she didn't need to choose between academic excellence and cultural authenticity— she could embody both simultaneously.

The Psychological Preparation Dynamic. The psychological preparation involved what many Black families call "dual consciousness development"—the ability to function effectively across multiple cultural contexts while maintaining a strong sense of self. This meant helping Jasmine understand that code-switching was not about being fake, but about being strategic (Hope et al., 2020; Ladson-Billings, 2021). When she spoke differently in different settings, she wasn't betraying her authentic self; she was demonstrating the kind of cultural competence that would serve her throughout her life.

From Individual Preparation to Family Mobilization

The strategy extended beyond individual preparation to family mobilization. When Jasmine faced challenges—whether they involved a teacher who consistently called on her to represent "the Black perspective" or classmates who questioned whether she deserved her place in advanced placement courses—her entire family mobilized. Her parents became strategic advocates; her older brother shared his experiences navigating predominantly white institutions; and her grandmother provided historical context that helped her understand her challenges as part of a larger story of progress and resistance. This comprehensive approach recognizes that thriving in challenging institutional environments requires more than individual grit: it demands systematic preparation, community support, and a clear understanding of both the obstacles and opportunities that lie ahead. Families who master this approach do not merely help their children survive; they also prepare them to transform the very institutions they enter.

The success of these strategies is evident in the countless Black professionals who credit their family's wisdom with helping them navigate challenging educational and professional environments: Some of these professional environments include the doctor who learned from her grandmother to document everything in writing when facing workplace discrimination; the engineer who absorbed his father's lessons about building coalitions across racial lines; and, the teacher who carries forward her mother's understanding that excellence is the best response to low expectations.

Building Armor Against Educational Racism

The metaphor of armor is particularly apt when discussing how Black families prepare their children for educational environments where racism, both subtle and overt, remains a persistent reality (Stevenson, 2014; Neblett et al., 2016). But this armor is not about becoming defensive or closed off—it is about developing the psychological, intellectual, and spiritual strength needed to maintain dignity and purpose in the face of systemic challenges.

Crafting and learning to use this armor begins early and involves multiple components: There is the intellectual armor that comes from understanding history and context—knowing that the challenges once faced are not personal failings but part of larger systemic patterns. Then, there is the emotional armor that comes from having a strong sense of self-worth that is not dependent on external validation. The social armor, moreover, that comes from being connected to communities affirms your value and potential. Finally, the spiritual armor comes from understanding your life as part of a larger purpose and calling.

Take the example of how Mrs. Rodriguez prepares her eight-year-old son, Antonio, for the realities he might face in his predominantly white elementary school. She doesn't begin with lectures about racism—instead, she starts with affirmation. Every morning, as she braids his hair or adjusts his backpack, she reminds him of his worth: "You are brilliant. You are loved. You belong in every space you enter. Your voice matters. Your ideas are valuable. "This daily affirmation ritual serves as the foundation for more complex conversations that unfold over time. When Antonio comes home confused about why his teacher seems to call on him less frequently than his white classmates, his mother doesn't dismiss his observation or tell him he's imagining things. Instead, she validates his experience while providing context and strategy. "Sometimes," she explains, "people make assumptions about what children like you can do. It's not right, and it's not about you—it's about ideas they learned that aren't true. Your job is to show them who you really are, not by being perfect, but by being yourself and working hard. And remember, even if one teacher doesn't see your brilliance, that doesn't make you any less brilliant."

This conversation, which imbeds several types of armor, does several things simultaneously: it acknowledges the reality of bias without making Antonio feel victimized; it provides him with a framework for understanding challenges he might face; it emphasizes his agency and power rather than his vulnerability; and it connects his individual experience to larger patterns without making him feel responsible for carrying the burden of representation.

The armor-building process also involves teaching children to distinguish between problems they can solve and systems they need to navigate strategically. When ten-year-old Keisha faces a teacher who consistently marks her down for "attitude" despite her exemplary behavior, her family does not just tell her to try harder, but they teach her to document interactions, to understand the difference between personal conflict and institutional bias, and to develop strategies for protecting herself while continuing to pursue excellence. Keisha therefore learns to carry a small notebook where she records positive interactions and achievements—not because she's paranoid, but because she's strategic. She learns to copy her parents on important emails to teachers, not because she can't handle things herself, but because she understands the power dynamics at play. She learns to celebrate her successes loudly and publicly, not because she's boastful, but because she understands that visibility can be protection.

The armor also includes what many families call "reality checks without dream crushing." Children learn about the existence of barriers without being overwhelmed by them. They understand that some challenges they face are unfair without being taught to expect unfairness in every situation. They develop the ability to assess situations accurately—neither naive about potential challenges nor paralyzed by anticipating problems that may not materialize.

This balanced approach is evident in the way families discuss college preparation and career planning. Parents don't hide the reality that their children might face additional scrutiny or need to work harder for the same recognition. But they also don't present these challenges as insurmountable obstacles. Instead, they frame them as factors to consider in strategic planning—like knowing you need to leave earlier for a destination because traffic might be heavy. The most sophisticated aspect of this armor-building process involves teaching children to maintain their sense of purpose and joy despite institutional challenges. The armor protects not

just against external attacks, but against internalized doubt and discouragement. Children learn that their worth is not determined by others' recognition, that their potential is not limited by others' imagination, and that their success is not dependent on others' approval.

Collective Healing and Resistance

The individual strategies for navigating institutional challenges are powerful, but they reach their full potential when embedded within communities committed to collective healing and resistance. Black families have long understood that the trauma inflicted by educational racism cannot be healed in isolation (Ginwright, 2018; Warren et al., 2009). Effectively dealing with the racism's traumatic aftermath requires community responses that address both individual wounds and systemic causes.

The concept of collective healing recognizes that when one child experiences discrimination in school, the entire community is affected.

When a bright student is tracked into lower-level courses because of biased assessments, it affects not just that student but their siblings, cousins, and neighborhood friends, who begin to doubt their own potential. When a family struggles to navigate a hostile school environment, other families learn to expect similar challenges.

In response to this reality, Black communities have developed sophisticated approaches to collective healing that operate at multiple levels. There are the informal networks of parents who share information about which teachers and administrators are supportive versus problematic. Church and community organization programs also provide academic support and college preparation, and mentorship programs connect young people with adults who have successfully navigated similar challenges in the Black community (Clemons, 2024).

Therapeutic Healing Strategy. The healing aspect of these circles was crucial. Parents who had internalized shame about their children's school struggles found community with others facing similar challenges. Children who had begun to doubt their abilities heard stories of other young people who had overcome obstacles and achieved success. Families discovered that their individual struggles were part of larger patterns that could be addressed through collective action.

The Resistance Strategy. The resistance component emerged naturally from the healing process. As families strengthened their relationships with one another, they also developed the capacity for advocacy. They learned to present a unified voice at school board meetings, to support one another during difficult conferences with administrators, and to celebrate each other's victories as community wins rather than individual achievements (Ishimaru, 2019; Engram Jr., 2023).

The Collective Strategy. The collective approach also involved what many communities call "protective programming"—creating alternative spaces where children could experience affirmation and high expectations, while building the skills needed to succeed in challenging institutional environments. These programs may have included Saturday academies that provided enrichment opportunities, summer camps that combined recreation with academic preparation, and after-school programs that offered both homework assistance and cultural education.

Moreover, the power of collective approaches becomes evident in measurable outcomes, such as improved academic achievement, reduced discipline disparities, increased parent engagement, and stronger school-community relationships. But the deeper impact lies in the transformation of community capacity—the development of networks, skills, and confidence that extend far beyond educational issues to encompass broader community development and social justice work. Even the families engaged in collective healing and resistance understand that their efforts serve multiple generations, addressing the immediate needs of their own children while building infrastructure and capacity that will benefit future generations, healing from past traumas while preventing future harm, and resisting current inequities while creating models for more just and effective educational approaches. This long-term perspective enables sustained commitment even when progress seems slow or setbacks occur. Families understand that institutional change happens gradually, that individual victories accumulate into community transformation, and that the armor they build for their children today becomes the foundation for the more welcoming institutions their grandchildren might inherit.

The wisdom embedded in these approaches to navigating institutional challenges reflects generations of learning about maintaining dignity and purpose in the face of adversity, transforming obstacles into opportunities, and building community strength that outlasts individual struggles. It represents a sophisticated understanding of how systemic change happens and how families can be agents of that change while protecting and nurturing their children. Ultimately, the strategies for surviving and thriving, the armor against educational racism, and the commitment to collective healing and resistance represent more than coping mechanisms—they constitute a blueprint for transformation that honors both individual potential and community strength. They remind us that the village that raises a classroom must be prepared not only to support children but also to challenge and change the systems that serve them, creating educational environments in which all children can flourish without sacrificing their authentic selves or community connections.

"If they don't give you a seat at the table, bring a folding chair." — **Shirley Chisholm**

CHAPTER EIGHT: COMMUNITY-BASED LEARNING MODELS

"Education is a communal activity." — **Carter G. Woodson**

Throughout Black communities, the sentiment remains consistent: when schools fail our children, we do not wait for permission to act. We gather in church basements, community centers, and living rooms. We teach what our children need to know, drawing from generations of wisdom and an unwavering commitment to their success. The African proverb "It takes a village to raise a child" finds its most practical expression in the educational spaces we create for ourselves. When traditional schools fall short of nurturing our children's full potential, Black communities have consistently responded by building our own learning environments. These spaces—born from necessity, sustained by love, and powered by collective wisdom—represent some of the most innovative and effective educational models in America.

Community-based learning acknowledges what we've always known: education extends far beyond classroom walls, and the most powerful learning happens when children see themselves reflected in their teachers, curriculum, and community. This understanding echoes long-standing critiques of schooling in Black communities that emphasize education as a collective project of racial uplift rather than merely individual advancement (Woodson, 1933). From the freedom schools of the 1960s (Watkins, 2001) to today's Saturday academies, from grandmother's kitchen table lessons to neighborhood study circles, we have created educational ecosystems that honor our children's brilliance while addressing their specific needs.

The Saturday School Revolution

Saturday schools emerged as a direct response to the limitations and biases of traditional public education (Ladson-Billings, 2021; Alim & Paris, 2017). These programs, typically held on weekends at churches, community centers, or schools, provide supplemental education that focuses on academic excellence, cultural pride, and character development. Unlike remedial programs designed to "catch up" struggling students, Saturday schools operate from a philosophy of abundance—recognizing and nurturing the gifts every child brings.

Children arrive each week eager to learn African history, practice advanced mathematics, and participate in coding workshops. Parents consistently report the transformation they witness: their children, who during the school week often come home frustrated and feeling unseen, transform on Saturdays. Surrounded by teachers who look like them, who understand their brilliance, and who challenge them to reach higher, these children rediscover their love of learning and sense of possibility.

Curriculum, Transformation, and Academic Rigor

The curriculum in these Saturday programs deliberately fills gaps left by traditional education. Children learn about the achievements of African civilizations, study the contributions of Black scientists and inventors, and engage with literature by authors who reflect their experiences. Learning goes beyond just representation: the strength of the curriculum also concentrates on providing the historical and cultural context that helps children understand their place in a larger narrative of resilience and achievement.

Educators who founded Saturday schools after their children struggled in traditional settings consistently describe witnessing remarkable transformations. Children who initially walk in with shoulders hunched and eyes down, believing what they have been told about their limitations, begin standing tall, asking questions, and challenging ideas within weeks, for they remember they are descendants of kings and queens, scientists and freedom fighters capable of academic success.

The academic rigor in these programs often exceeds what children experience during the regular school week. In fact, teachers, many of whom are education professionals volunteering their time, create challenging, culturally relevant curricula that push students to excel. Children might study advanced mathematics through African geometric patterns, explore scientific concepts through traditional healing practices, or develop writing skills by crafting stories that center Black experiences.

After-School Sanctuaries

While Saturday schools provide intensive weekend learning, after-school programs serve as daily bridges between home and school, offering academic support, enrichment activities, and crucial mentorship. These programs, often housed in community centers, libraries, churches, or recreation facilities, create safe spaces where children can decompress from challenging school days while engaging in meaningful learning experiences.

Positive Outcomes. Many after-school programs exemplify the power of community-based programming (Lester et al., 2020). Founded by retired teachers in church basements and community centers, these programs now serve hundreds of students from kindergarten through high school. Students receive homework help, participate in book clubs, learn musical instruments, engage in community service projects, and develop leadership skills through mentoring younger children. Program directors consistently emphasize that their work extends far beyond homework assistance. They help children understand that they belong in advanced classes, that they can pursue any career they dream of, that their voices matter. Half of their work focuses on academics, while the other half involves healing the damage done during regular school days.

The program's success stories are numerous: students who moved from failing grades to honor roll, young people who discovered talents in areas never explored in their regular schools, teenagers who found the confidence to apply to college. But perhaps most importantly, these programs provide community connections that sustain families through difficult times. When young people face family crises, these learning centers become their anchor. Volunteer mentors step in to provide role models, older students offer peer support, and program directors connect families with resources for counseling and assistance. Parents frequently express that these programs saved their children, providing stable ground when everything else was falling apart and ensuring their children had somewhere to go where people believed in them.

After-school programs also serve as training grounds for young leaders. High school students mentor younger children, developing teaching and leadership skills while earning community service hours. College students return to volunteer, creating pathways of inspiration and practical guidance. Adults in the community share their professional expertise, exposing children to career possibilities they might not otherwise encounter.

Informal Learning Networks

Beyond formal programs, Black communities have always maintained informal networks of learning and support (*González* et al., 2005; Ishimaru, 2019). These networks have included grandmother's math lessons at the kitchen table, older cousin's reading sessions on the front porch, neighbor's career conversations over the fence--all representing a parallel education system that operates largely invisibly but with tremendous impact. Even sister circles, book clubs, and neighborhood study groups create spaces in which parents share educational resources, discuss advocacy strategies, and support one another through school challenges. These networks often serve as early warning systems, alerting families to issues like biased teachers, inadequate resources, or inappropriate special education referrals.

Many families exemplify how these informal networks operate. When children begin struggling with reading or mathematics, families don't wait for the school's response. Grandmothers create home libraries filled with culturally relevant books. College-bound siblings provide daily tutoring sessions. Neighbors who are former teachers share educational games and strategies. By working together, children often achieve academic success that schools predicted was impossible. The philosophy underlying these networks remains consistent across communities: families know that waiting for schools to address problems often means children fall further behind. Instead, they activate their village, with everyone contributing what they can—time, expertise, resources, encouragement. This approach reflects how Black communities have always survived and thrived.

These networks also preserve and transmit cultural knowledge that formal education often neglects. Children learn family histories, traditional crafts, storytelling techniques, and survival strategies passed down through generations. They understand their connection to a larger community and develop the confidence that comes from knowing they are valued and supported. Technology has expanded the reach and effectiveness of these networks. WhatsApp groups allow parents to share homework help and study resources instantly. Facebook pages connect families facing similar educational challenges. Virtual tutoring sessions enable relatives in different cities to support children's learning. Video calls bring distant elders into children's daily educational experiences.

Creating Our Own Educational Spaces

The ultimate expression of community-based learning is the creation of entirely new educational institutions designed specifically for Black children. These schools, whether traditional private schools, charter schools, homeschool cooperatives, or alternative learning communities, represent the boldest assertion of educational self-determination (Love, 2019; Ladson-Billings, 2021). Community schools emerge from groups of frustrated parents who decide to stop fighting the system and create their own. Working with educators, community leaders, and cultural practitioners, they develop schools that integrate academic excellence with cultural affirmation, social justice education, and community engagement. These schools' curricula include standard subjects taught through African-centered perspectives, as well as courses in African languages, traditional arts, community organizing, and entrepreneurship. Students engage in service-learning projects that address real community needs, ranging from environmental justice campaigns to elder care programs. By graduation, students have not only mastered academic content but also developed strong cultural identities and leadership skills.

Educators and administrators at these schools consistently emphasize their broader mission beyond college and career preparation. They focus on preparing children to be healers and leaders in their communities, to carry forward the best of their traditions while creating new possibilities for future generations. Homeschool cooperatives represent another model of community-created education. Groups of families pool resources to hire teachers, rent spaces, and develop curricula that serve their children's specific needs. These cooperatives often focus on accelerated academics, cultural education, and individualized learning approaches that recognize different learning styles and paces.

Learning cooperatives across the country serve families who want alternatives to both traditional public schools and predominantly white private schools. Meeting several days per week in rented church spaces, children receive instruction in core subjects while participating in art workshops, music lessons, and field trips to historically Black colleges and universities. Cooperative founders consistently express their motivation in similar terms: their children are brilliant, but traditional schools were damaging them by failing to see their gifts. In cooperative settings, every child is celebrated for their unique talents while being challenged to reach their highest potential. These parents have created the schools they wish had existed when they were children.

The Divine Nine: Pillars of Educational Excellence

The nine historically Black Greek-letter organizations—Alpha Phi Alpha, Alpha Kappa Alpha, Kappa Alpha Psi, Omega Psi Phi, Delta Sigma Theta, Phi Beta Sigma, Zeta Phi Beta, Sigma Gamma Rho, and Iota Phi Theta—represent one of the most powerful and sustained examples of community-based educational support in Black America (Ross, 2016). Known collectively as the Divine Nine, these organizations have been foundational in creating and maintaining educational opportunities for over a century. From their founding in the early 1900s to the present, these fraternities and sororities have operated on the principle that education is both a personal achievement and a community responsibility. Their members—doctors, lawyers, teachers, engineers, business leaders, and public servants—return to their communities not just as successful individuals but as resources committed to lifting others.

The educational programming of the Divine Nine extends across all age groups and academic levels. For young children, they sponsor reading programs, math competitions, and cultural enrichment activities. Elementary students participate in oratorical contests that build confidence and public speaking skills while celebrating Black history and achievement. Middle and high school students participate in mentorship programs, college-preparation workshops, and leadership development initiatives. College readiness, in particular, has been a focus, with organizations offering SAT preparation courses, college application assistance, scholarship programs, and campus visits to historically Black colleges and universities. These efforts recognize that academic preparation alone is insufficient—students also need guidance in navigating college systems, financial aid processes, and career planning.

The scholarship programs of the Divine Nine have supported thousands of students who might otherwise lack access to higher education. But these aren't simply financial transactions; they represent investments in future community leaders. Scholarship recipients are expected to give back, creating cycles of support that strengthen over generations. Mentorship within the Divine Nine operates through formal programs and informal networks. Young people are paired with professionals who provide academic guidance, career advice, and personal support. These relationships often extend far beyond formal program periods, creating lifelong connections that benefit both mentors and mentees. The organizations also address educational challenges that extend beyond individual student needs. They advocate for improved school facilities, fair funding formulas, and equitable educational policies (Engram Jr., 2023; Ross, 2016). They provide professional development for teachers, particularly those working in underserved communities. They create partnerships with schools to supplement resources and programming.

During the civil rights era, the Divine Nine played crucial roles in educational desegregation efforts while simultaneously strengthening Black educational institutions. Members participated in voter registration drives, school integration efforts, and advocacy for educational equity. They provided safe spaces for planning and organizing while maintaining their commitment to educational excellence. Today, the Divine Nine continues to evolve its educational mission to address contemporary challenges. They sponsor STEM programs to increase Black participation in science and technology fields. They provide financial literacy education to help families build wealth and invest in education. They develop entrepreneurship programs that teach young people to view themselves as job creators rather than merely job seekers.

The graduate chapters of these organizations serve as bridges between educational institutions and communities. Members working in education bring resources and expertise back to their chapters, while those in other professions contribute skills and connections that benefit educational initiatives. This cross-pollination creates comprehensive support systems that address multiple barriers to educational success.

The Divine Nine's approach to education emphasizes both individual achievement and collective advancement. They celebrate academic excellence while recognizing that true success requires community engagement and social responsibility. Their members understand that their degrees and professional achievements carry obligations to future generations. Perhaps most importantly, the Divine Nine provides models of educational achievement that young people can see and touch. Children and teenagers regularly interact with Black professionals who demonstrate that educational success is both possible and valued within their communities. They see doctors who grew up in similar neighborhoods, lawyers who faced similar challenges, and teachers who understand their experiences.

The cultural programming of these organizations also serves educational purposes, teaching young people about Black history, traditions, and values that formal education often omits. Step shows, cultural celebrations, and community service projects serve as vehicles for transmitting knowledge and fostering pride. As community-based learning continues to evolve, the Divine Nine's century-long commitment to education provides both inspiration and practical models. Their combination of direct service, advocacy, mentorship, and resource development demonstrates how organizations can create comprehensive educational support systems that strengthen both individuals and communities.

The Ripple Effects of Community Learning

Community-based learning models create benefits that extend far beyond individual student achievement: These programs strengthen family engagement with education, build social capital within neighborhoods, and create pathways for community members to contribute their skills and knowledge to the next generation. Parents who participate in these programs often become more effective advocates for their children in traditional school settings (Warren et al., 2009; Ishimaru, 2019). They develop a deeper understanding of educational concepts, build relationships with other families facing similar challenges, and gain confidence to challenge inequitable practices. Many parents report that their involvement in community learning programs transformed their own relationship with education. Parents also frequently report feeling intimidated upon entering their children's schools, but after volunteering in community programs and seeing how education could look differently, they find their voice. They become unafraid to ask questions, to demand better, to speak up when something isn't right.

In addition to parental involvement, young people who participate in these programs often become community leaders themselves. They return as volunteers and mentors, start their own educational initiatives, and carry forward the values of collective responsibility and educational excellence, creating a cycle of community investment that strengthens over time. The programs also serve as testing grounds for innovative educational approaches that influence broader educational reform. Teaching methods developed in Saturday schools are adopted in public school classrooms. In fact, curricula created by community educators are adopted by traditional institutions. Even the leadership development and advocacy skills nurtured in these spaces drive policy changes at district and state levels.

Challenges and Sustainability

Despite their successes, community-based learning programs face significant challenges. Funding is often precarious, dependent on volunteer labor and small donations. Space can be difficult to secure, with programs moving frequently as rental costs rise or partnerships change, and teacher retention is challenging when most instructors are volunteers with other professional obligations.

The emotional labor required to sustain these programs is also enormous. Founders and leaders, predominantly Black women, often work multiple jobs while dedicating weekends and evenings to programming. Burnout is common, and succession planning is frequently inadequate. Longtime program directors consistently express the same concerns: they give everything they have because they know their children's futures depend on it, but they wonder who will carry this work forward when they can no longer do it. The need for younger people to step up and for real resources to make this work sustainable remains a pressing challenge. Additionally, competition with other weekend activities also poses challenges. As children get older, sports leagues, social events, and family obligations often interfere with program attendance. Some programs have adapted by offering more flexible scheduling, incorporating recreational activities, or partnering with sports organizations to create complementary programming.

Building for the Future

The future of community-based learning lies in better coordination, increased resources, and broader recognition of these programs' value. Forming to share best practices, coordinate programming, and advocate for public funding, community-based networks are taking the lead in this area. Technology platforms are also being developed to connect programs across geographic boundaries and facilitate resource sharing. Even some communities are exploring formal partnerships with school districts, creating community schools that blend traditional and community-based approaches. Others are pursuing social enterprise models, developing revenue streams that reduce dependence on donations while maintaining focus on community service.

Despite the challenges posed by the COVID-19 pandemic, community-based learning programs demonstrated resilience and innovation (Darling-Hammond & Hyler, 2020). Many quickly adapted to online formats, created learning pods for children of essential workers, and provided crucial support during school closures. These experiences have strengthened the case for greater recognition and support of community education initiatives. Young adults who grew up in these programs are now returning as professional educators, nonprofit leaders, and community organizers. They bring fresh perspectives on program sustainability, youth engagement, and community partnerships. Their leadership ensures that community-based learning continues to evolve to meet new challenges while maintaining its core values of cultural affirmation and educational excellence.

The Village in Action

Community-based learning models represent the village principle in its most practical and powerful form. When schools fail our children, we do not wait for permission to act . Instead we gather our resources, marshal our expertise, and create the educational experiences our children deserve. These efforts require sacrifice, creativity, and unwavering commitment, but they produce results that justify every investment. The children who participate in these programs do more than just achieve academic success: they develop strong cultural identities, leadership skills, and community connections that serve them throughout their lives. They understand that education is not something done to them, but something they actively participate in creating. They ultimately see themselves as inheritors of a rich intellectual tradition and contributors to their community's ongoing development.

As we look toward the future of education, community-based learning models offer crucial insights, such as demonstrating that effective education requires cultural relevance, community engagement, and recognition of students' strengths rather than a fixation on deficits, and showing that parents and community members are not barriers to educational excellence but essential partners in creating it. Most importantly, these programs embody the truth that has sustained Black communities through centuries of struggle: when the systems around us fail, we have the power to create new ones. We have always been our own salvation, and in the realm of education, we continue to build the schools, programs, and learning communities that will nurture the next generation of leaders, healers, and change-makers.

The village that raises our children includes entire communities committed to educational excellence beyond just individual family members. In Saturday schools and after-school programs, in informal learning networks and newly created educational spaces, that village continues its essential work, ensuring that every child has access to the transformative power of education rooted in love, grounded in culture, and dedicated to their unlimited potential.

The strength of the Black community has always been its ability to come together.
— Dr. Martin Luther King Jr.

CHAPTER NINE: INTERGENERATIONAL TRAUMA AND HEALING

"History is not the past. It is the present. We carry our history with us. We are our history."
— **James Baldwin**

The wounds of educational exclusion run deep in Black families, carrying stories that span generations. From grandparents who were denied the right to read, to parents who faced hostile school environments, to children navigating contemporary forms of educational discrimination, the trauma of being told we are less capable, less worthy, less intelligent creates lasting impacts that affect how families approach learning and schools. Yet within these same families lies extraordinary resilience and wisdom about healing. Black communities have always understood that education involves not just the mind but the whole person—emotions, spirit, cultural identity, and sense of belonging. This holistic understanding provides the foundation for addressing educational trauma while building learning environments that nurture rather than harm.

Understanding intergenerational trauma in education requires recognizing that many Black families carry complex relationships with formal schooling. These relationships are shaped by historical exclusion, ongoing discrimination, and the persistent need to navigate systems that were not designed for our success. At the same time, education has always represented hope, opportunity, and liberation in Black communities. This tension—between education as trauma and education as salvation—influences how families approach their children's learning experiences.

The effects of anti-Blackness in education accumulate across generations, shaping not only academic trajectories but emotional relationships to schools themselves. Historical exclusion from literacy and segregated schooling—documented in seminal educational histories (Anderson, 1988)—combine with contemporary racialized discipline regimes and deficit narratives to produce collective memories of harm that surface as vigilance, mistrust, or protective distancing from institutions (Dumas, 2016; Love, 2019). Yet Black families simultaneously transmit healing practices: storytelling that restores worth, faith traditions that anchor hope, community mentors who intervene before systems fail, and rituals that reaffirm brilliance after institutional injury (Ginwright, 2018). Understanding intergenerational trauma therefore requires holding two truths at once—the persistence of anti-Black educational structures and the enduring capacity of Black communities to generate care, meaning, and possibility in spite of them.

Understanding the Emotional Landscapes of Learning

Educational trauma manifests itself in countless ways within Black families. In fact, parents who were labeled as slow learners or troublemakers may struggle with feelings of inadequacy when helping their children with homework. Students who face microaggressions, lower expectations, or cultural invalidation in classrooms may also develop negative associations with learning itself. Likewise, families may experience anxiety around school interactions, fear of advocating for their children, or resignation about educational possibilities.

The impacts of educational trauma extend beyond individual experiences to shape family dynamics around learning. Some parents become hypervigilant about their children's academic performance, driven by fear that any struggle will confirm negative stereotypes. Others may withdraw from school involvement, feeling ill-equipped to navigate systems that historically excluded them. Children may internalize messages about their intellectual limitations, developing learned helplessness or academic anxiety that persists throughout their educational journey. These emotional landscapes are further complicated by the intersection of race, class, and other identities (Crenshaw, 1989). Families navigating poverty may experience additional stress around accessing educational resources. Parents who are themselves dealing with trauma—

from racism, economic instability, or other life challenges—may struggle to provide the emotional support their children need for academic success. Single parents may feel overwhelmed by the demands of both earning income and managing their children's educational needs.

The cumulative impact of these experiences can create what some educators call educational PTSD—a persistent state of hypervigilance, anxiety, and emotional dysregulation around academic settings. Children may experience physical symptoms like headaches or stomachaches before school, have difficulty concentrating in classroom environments, or exhibit behavioral challenges that are actually trauma responses rather than defiance or inability. Understanding these emotional landscapes requires recognizing that resistance to education often represents self-protection rather than lack of interest in learning. When children shut down in classrooms, avoid homework, or act out during academic activities, they may be responding to environments that feel psychologically unsafe. When parents seem disengaged from school activities, they may be protecting themselves from repeated experiences of being marginalized or dismissed.

The impact of educational trauma also extends to how families view their own knowledge and capabilities. Parents who struggled in traditional school settings may doubt their ability to support their children's learning, despite possessing valuable knowledge and skills. Grandparents who were denied educational opportunities may feel intimidated by modern academic expectations, even though they have wisdom and experience that could greatly benefit their grandchildren's development. Children absorb these family dynamics around education, often internalizing negative beliefs about learning and their own capabilities before they even begin formal schooling. They may arrive at school already carrying the weight of generational educational trauma, making them more vulnerable to additional harm and less resilient in the face of academic challenges.

Therapeutic Approaches to Education

Healing educational trauma requires approaches that address both individual and systemic factors. Therapeutic education recognizes that learning happens most effectively in environments that feel emotionally safe, culturally affirming, and personally meaningful. This approach prioritizes relationship-building, trauma-informed practices, and holistic support for students and families.

Trauma-informed Educational Practices. Trauma-informed educational practices begin with understanding how trauma affects learning and behavior. Educators trained in trauma-informed approaches recognize that disruptive behavior may indicate emotional distress rather than willful defiance. They create classroom environments that prioritize safety, predictability, and positive relationships. They understand that healing must precede or accompany learning for many students who have experienced educational trauma (Crosby et al, 2018; Overstreet & Chafouleas, 2016).

Emotionally Safe Learning Environments. Creating emotionally safe learning environments involves establishing clear expectations, consistent routines, and multiple opportunities for students to experience success. Teachers focus on building relationships with students, understanding their individual needs and strengths, and creating learning experiences that connect to students' lives and interests. They recognize that academic growth may be slow for students healing from trauma and adjust expectations accordingly.

Culturally Sustaining Pedagogy. Culturally sustaining pedagogy serves as a therapeutic approach by validating students' identities and experiences. When children see themselves reflected in curriculum, when their cultural knowledge is valued and incorporated into learning, when their communities' contributions are celebrated rather than ignored, the healing process begins. This approach helps repair the damage caused by educational practices that position Black culture and knowledge as deficient or irrelevant (Paris & Alim, 2017; Muhammad, 2020).

Therapeutic Education and Family Engagement. Family engagement in therapeutic education requires rebuilding trust between schools and Black families. This process involves acknowledging past harm, demonstrating a genuine commitment to change, and creating multiple pathways for family involvement that honor different comfort levels and levels of expertise. Schools may need to provide healing opportunities for parents as well as children, recognizing that family trauma affects the entire educational ecosystem.

Social-Emotional Learning. Social-emotional learning becomes particularly important for students healing from educational trauma. These programs teach emotional regulation, conflict resolution, and relationship skills while helping students develop positive self-concepts and cultural pride. However, effective social-emotional learning for Black students must be culturally responsive and trauma-informed, avoiding deficit-based approaches that pathologize normal responses to discrimination and marginalization (Jagers et al., 2025).

Restorative Practice Alternatives. Restorative practices offer alternatives to punitive discipline that can retraumatize students. Instead of suspension and punishment, restorative approaches focus on repairing harm, building understanding, and strengthening community. These practices recognize that behavioral challenges often stem from unmet needs or trauma responses and work to address root causes rather than just symptoms (Gregory et al., 2016; Anyon et al., 2016).

Mental Health Support. Mental health support becomes essential for addressing educational trauma, but traditional therapeutic approaches may not be culturally responsive to Black students' needs. Effective therapeutic interventions incorporate understanding of racism, cultural identity development, and community resilience. They recognize that some symptoms labeled as pathological may actually represent healthy responses to unhealthy environments.

Peer Support and Mentorship Programs. Peer support and mentorship programs connect students with others who have faced similar challenges and overcome them. These relationships provide hope, practical strategies, and emotional support while helping students develop positive identity and future orientation. Mentors who share students' racial and cultural backgrounds can be particularly effective in addressing educational trauma.

Creative and Expressive Therapies. Creative and expressive therapies—including art, music, dance, and storytelling—provide alternative pathways for processing trauma and expressing experiences that may be difficult to verbalize. These approaches honor African cultural traditions that have always used creative expression for healing and meaning-making.

Breaking Cycles of Educational Harm

Interrupting intergenerational educational trauma requires intentional efforts to heal past wounds while creating new, positive experiences around learning. This process involves working with entire families, not just individual students, to address the complex ways that educational trauma affects family systems.

Healing the Family. Family healing begins with creating safe spaces for parents and caregivers to process their own educational experiences. Many adults carry shame, anger, or fear related to their schooling that affects how they interact with their children's education. Support groups, counseling services, and family education programs that acknowledge and address these experiences can help parents heal while developing skills to support their children differently. Reframing family narratives around education becomes crucial for breaking cycles of harm. Families may need support in recognizing their strengths, acknowledging the systemic barriers they have faced, and developing new stories about their relationship with learning. This process involves helping family members understand that academic struggles often reflect inadequate systems rather than personal failures.

Building Skills in Educational Advocacy. Building educational advocacy skills empowers families to navigate school systems more effectively while protecting their children from harm. Advocacy training helps parents understand their rights, develop communication strategies, and build confidence in challenging inappropriate practices. This knowledge can transform families from feeling powerless within educational systems to becoming effective advocates for their children.

Creating Positive Learning Experiences Beyond the School Setting. Creating positive learning experiences outside of traditional school settings allows families to rebuild their relationship with education in supportive environments. Saturday schools, homeschool cooperatives, cultural programs, and family learning activities can help children and parents experience the joy of learning together without the stress and trauma associated with traditional school settings.

Developing Cultural Pride and Positive Racial Self Esteem. Developing cultural pride and positive racial identity serves as protection against educational trauma. When children have strong cultural foundations and positive self-concepts, they are more resilient in the face of bias and discrimination. They understand that negative treatment reflects systemic problems rather than personal inadequacies.

History as Enlightenment and Blueprint for Constructive Resistance. Teaching children about the history of educational exclusion and resistance helps them contextualize their experiences within larger patterns of struggle and triumph. Understanding that their ancestors fought for the right to learn, that education has always been valued in Black communities despite barriers, and that they are part of a legacy of resilience can transform how children view academic challenges.

Constructing Family-Oriented Intergenerational Bridges. Building intergenerational bridges within families allows knowledge and wisdom to flow between generations in healing ways. Grandparents who were denied educational opportunities can share their life wisdom and cultural knowledge. Parents can model learning and growth while acknowledging their own struggles.

Children can share their educational experiences while learning from their elders' resilience. Creating networks of support among families facing similar challenges reduces isolation and builds collective power. When families connect with others who understand their experiences, they develop strategies for healing while building community advocacy efforts. These networks can also provide practical support like tutoring, childcare, and resource sharing.

Systems Change as a Vehicle for Healing and Educational Transformation. Engaging in systems change work helps families channel their healing energy into transforming the educational institutions that have caused harm. Parent organizing, policy advocacy, and community education efforts not only create better conditions for all children but provide therapeutic benefits for families who transform from victims of educational trauma to agents of educational change (Hope et al., 2020).

The Divine Nine: Models of Healing and Excellence

Historically Black Greek-letter organizations have long recognized the connection between healing and educational achievement. Through their programming and community engagement, these organizations address educational trauma while creating pathways to success.

Mentorship. The mentorship programs of the Divine Nine provide healing relationships for young people who may have experienced educational harm. These mentors, who have often overcome similar challenges, model resilience while providing practical support and emotional guidance. They help young people reframe their educational experiences and develop positive academic identities.

Scholarship and Recognition. Scholarship and recognition programs celebrate academic achievement while addressing the imposter syndrome that many Black students experience. By honoring excellence within Black communities, these programs counter messages of intellectual inferiority while providing financial support that makes educational dreams possible.

Cultural Programming. Cultural programming helps young people develop pride in their heritage while understanding their place within a legacy of educational achievement. Step shows, oratorical contests, and cultural celebrations create positive associations with learning and community engagement.

Service Learning. Service learning initiatives connect education to community improvement, helping young people understand that their learning serves purposes beyond individual advancement. This connection to community healing and empowerment can transform education from a source of trauma to a tool for liberation. The professional networks within the Divine Nine provide career guidance and opportunity while demonstrating that educational success is possible for Black students. Seeing lawyers, doctors, teachers, and business leaders who share their background helps young people envision positive futures while providing practical pathways to achievement.

Alumni Engagement. Alumni engagement creates cycles of support where those who have benefited from educational opportunities return to support the next generation. This intergenerational investment helps heal educational trauma while building sustainable systems of support.

Healing-Centered Educational Practices

Moving beyond trauma-informed approaches, healing-centered education actively promotes wellness and resilience while addressing the root causes of educational harm. These approaches recognize that healing is not just the absence of trauma but the presence of positive conditions that support holistic development.

Healing-Centered Classrooms. Healing-centered classrooms prioritize relationships, community, and belonging. Students learn about their cultural heritage while developing academic skills. They engage in collaborative learning that builds social connections while mastering content. They participate in service learning that connects their education to community improvement.

Culturally Sustaining Curriculum. Culturally sustaining curriculum not only includes Black history and contributions but positions Black knowledge systems as valuable and relevant. Students learn about African philosophical traditions, traditional healing practices, historical achievements, and contemporary innovations. This approach counters deficit narratives while building positive cultural identity.

Mindfulness and Meditation Practices. Mindfulness and meditation practices, adapted for cultural relevance, help students develop emotional regulation and stress management skills. These practices may incorporate African spiritual traditions, hip hop music, or other culturally relevant elements that resonate with Black students' experiences.

Community Partnerships. Community partnerships bring healing professionals, cultural practitioners, and community elders into educational settings. These partnerships expand the resources available for addressing trauma while connecting students to broader support networks.

Family Engagement Strategies. Family engagement strategies acknowledge the need for healing relationships between schools and Black families. These efforts may include family therapy services, parent support groups, and cultural programming that brings families together around positive educational experiences.

Restorative Justice Practices. Restorative justice practices create opportunities for healing when harm occurs within educational settings. Rather than simply punishing students for behavioral infractions, these practices focus on understanding root causes, repairing relationships, and building stronger community.

The Ripple Effects of Educational Healing

When families heal from educational trauma, the benefits extend far beyond individual academic achievement. Children who experience healing-centered education are more likely to become confident learners, effective advocates, and community leaders. They develop resilience that serves them throughout their lives while building positive relationships with learning that they pass on to their own children. Likewise, parents who heal from their own educational trauma become more effective supporters of their children's learning. They develop confidence in their ability to navigate educational systems while building positive relationships with schools and teachers. They are more likely to advocate for their children and engage in school improvement efforts.

Communities benefit when families heal from educational trauma because healed individuals are more likely to contribute their talents and leadership to community development. They become teachers, mentors, and advocates who work to improve educational opportunities for all children. The healing process also creates new knowledge about effective educational practices. Families who have navigated healing journeys develop expertise that can inform educational policy and practice. Their experiences provide valuable insights into what works and what causes harm in educational settings.

Sustaining Healing and Preventing Retraumatization

Long-term healing requires sustained commitment to practices and policies that prevent re-traumatization while continuing to promote wellness. These practices and policies involve ongoing professional development for educators, continuous family support services, and systemic changes that address root causes of educational harm. Professional development for educators must include training in trauma-informed practices, cultural responsiveness, and healing-centered approaches. Teachers need ongoing support to examine their biases, develop cultural competence, and create classrooms that support healing rather than perpetuate harm.

Family support services must likewise be sustained and accessible, recognizing that healing is an ongoing process rather than a one-time intervention. Families may need different types of support at different times, and services must be flexible and responsive to changing needs. Policy changes at the school, district, and state levels can also create systemic conditions that support healing while preventing trauma. These changes may include discipline policy reforms, funding for mental health services, requirements for cultural responsiveness training, and accountability measures that track emotional and social outcomes alongside academic achievement.

Community partnerships must be authentic and sustained, built on mutual respect and a shared commitment to children's well-being. These partnerships should include healing professionals, cultural practitioners, community organizations, and families as equal partners in creating supportive educational environments.

The Path Forward

Healing intergenerational educational trauma is not just about addressing past harm but about creating new possibilities for future generations. When we understand the emotional landscapes of learning, implement therapeutic approaches to education, and actively work to break cycles of harm, we create conditions for Black children and families to thrive educationally.

This healing work requires acknowledging the reality of educational trauma while refusing to be defined by it. It involves honoring the pain that families have experienced while celebrating their resilience and strength. It means creating educational environments that see Black children as brilliant, capable, and deserving of the very best education possible. The healing process transforms not just individuals and families but entire communities. When Black children experience education as affirming rather than traumatic, when families feel welcomed rather than marginalized in schools, when communities see education as liberation rather than oppression, the ripple effects extend throughout society.

Ultimately, healing intergenerational educational trauma is about reclaiming education as a tool for empowerment rather than oppression. It means creating learning environments where every Black child can thrive academically while developing strong cultural identity and community connections. It requires recognizing that true educational excellence cannot be achieved without addressing the emotional, cultural, and spiritual dimensions of learning.

This healing work continues the legacy of ancestors who understood that education and liberation are intimately connected. It honors their sacrifices while creating new possibilities for future generations. In healing educational trauma, we not only transform individual lives but also contribute to the broader struggle for educational justice and racial equity.

In the final analysis, the village that raises our children must also heal our children. By understanding trauma, implementing healing practices, and breaking cycles of harm, we create educational environments in which every child can discover and develop their gifts. This is not just educational reform—it is liberation work that transforms communities and creates new possibilities for future generations.

Rarely, if ever, are any of us, healed in isolation. Healing is an act of communion. — **bell hooks**

CHAPTER TEN: THE WAY FORWARD

"Education is our passport to the future, for tomorrow belongs to the people who prepare for it today." - **Malcolm X**

Reimagining What Education Can Be

For generations, Black families have understood what mainstream education is only beginning to discover: it truly takes a village to raise a child, and by extension, it takes a village to raise a classroom. Our ancestors knew that learning happens everywhere—in kitchens where mathematics lives in measurements and ratios, on front porches where storytelling preserves history and builds character, in churches where oratory skills are honed, and community values are transmitted, and in extended family networks where each elder becomes a teacher and each child a precious vessel of potential. This ancestral wisdom points toward an educational future that honors the full spectrum of how Black children learn best—through relationship, through relevance, through rhythm, and through resistance to systems that would diminish their brilliance (Paris & Alim, 2017; Love, 2019).

Learning Rooted in Community Wisdom

Imagine educational environments that begin with the understanding that every child comes from a community rich with knowledge, even when that knowledge isn't recognized by traditional academic institutions (*González* et al., 2005; Llopart & Esteban-Guitart, 2018). In these spaces, a grandmother's quilting becomes a geometry class, a grandfather's barbershop stories become social studies, and a parent's code-switching expertise becomes advanced linguistics.

These learning communities recognize that academic excellence and cultural authenticity aren't opposing forces but complementary strengths

(Paris & Alim, 2017; Love, 2019). Students studying African American literature don't just analyze texts—they connect with living griots in their communities, learning how oral tradition shapes the written word. When exploring mathematics, they discover the geometric principles in African art, the mathematical foundations of jazz improvisation, and the statistical strategies that powered the Underground Railroad.

The curriculum becomes a mirror that reflects students' heritage while simultaneously preparing them for any future they choose to pursue. This isn't about lowering standards or creating separate educational tracks—it's about raising standards by honoring the full range of human intelligence and cultural knowledge that students bring to their learning.

The Power of Collective Achievement

Black families have always understood that individual success is meaningless without uplifting the community. This wisdom transforms how we think about academic achievement. Instead of fostering competition that pits students against one another, future learning environments emphasize collective success, in which each person's growth contributes to everyone's advancement (Paris & Alim, 2017). Consider mathematics circles in which older students mentor younger students, creating chains of learning that strengthen the entire community. Envision science labs in which students not only conduct experiments but also design solutions to challenges facing their neighborhoods—from environmental justice issues to health disparities (Maier et al., 2017). Imagine history classes in which students not only study the civil rights movement but also organize contemporary social justice initiatives and understand themselves as part of an ongoing struggle for equity. In these environments, the question isn't "Who's the smartest?" but "How can we all get smarter together?" Success is measured not by individual test scores but by collective growth, community contribution, and the strengthening of bonds that will support students long after they leave the classroom.

Culturally Sustaining Pedagogy

The educational future we envision goes beyond tolerating cultural differences to celebrating and building upon them (Paris & Alim, 2017).

Black students are not asked or required to choose between academic success and cultural identity because the learning environment honors both as essential components of human development.

Call-and-response becomes a teaching method that engages students' natural rhythms. Storytelling traditions inform both literature classes and scientific hypothesis formation. The collaborative learning styles that reflect African communal values shape classroom structures. Students see themselves reflected not only in isolated units on Black history but also throughout the curriculum as mathematicians, scientists, artists, leaders, and innovators. This approach recognizes that when students can bring their full selves to learning—their language, their experiences, their ways of knowing—they perform at higher levels because they're operating from a place of strength rather than deficit (Paris & Alim, 2017; Love, 2019).

For too long, Black children have been subjected to educational approaches that pathologize their culture, criminalize their behavior, and underestimate their potential. The future we envision breaks free from these limiting narratives, creating a new world in which the embedded brilliance of Black communities, far too overlooked and suppressed, can flourish

Changing the School-to-Prison Pipeline Trajectory

The current educational system often functions as a pathway that funnels Black children toward incarceration rather than graduation (Dumas, 2016; Love, 2019). The future we're building creates school-to-success pipelines that recognize potential where others see problems, respond to trauma with healing rather than punishment, and recognize that behavioral challenges often mask academic gifts.

Restorative justice practices should replace zero-tolerance policies, creating environments in which conflicts become learning opportunities and mistakes become growth experiences (Davison et al., 2021). Counselors and social workers outnumber security guards, and mental health support is as readily available as academic tutoring. Schools become healing spaces that address the impact of systemic racism while building resilience and strength (Ginwright, 2018). In these environments, a child's passion might be channeled into positive leadership rather than seen as defiance. A student's questioning of authority might be recognized as critical thinking skills rather than labeled as disrespect. The energy that traditional schools try to suppress becomes the fuel for engaged learning and community leadership.

Transcending the Achievement Gap Narrative

The persistent focus on achievement gaps has trained us to see Black students in terms of what they lack rather than what they bring. The future of education reverses this deficit-based thinking, focusing on opportunity gaps that prevent students from accessing quality education and, more importantly, on excellence gaps that fail to recognize the forms of brilliance that do not show up on standardized tests (Dumas, 2016; Love, 2019).

Instead of constantly measuring how far behind Black students are, future learning communities should measure how much growth is happening, how much joy is present in learning, how much community is being built, and how much positive change students are creating in their neighborhoods. Assessment becomes about documenting strength and potential rather than ranking and sorting (Paris & Alim, 2017). This shift requires educators to broaden their definition of intelligence to include emotional intelligence, cultural intelligence, social intelligence, and creative intelligence—areas in which many Black students excel but that traditional schools often undervalue.

Liberating Learning from White Supremacist Structures

Much of what we accept as "normal" in education actually reflects white cultural values and learning styles presented as universal truths (Dumas, 2016; Love, 2019). A better future for education for Black students requires recognizing this cultural bias and creating space for diverse ways of knowing and being.

Collaborative learning then becomes as valued as individual achievement. Oral presentation skills receive the same attention as written communication (Paris & Alim, 2017). Movement and music become learning tools rather than distractions. Extended family and community members are welcomed as educational partners rather than as sources of interference. This liberation does not mean lowering standards. Rather, it means expanding our understanding of what excellence looks like and creating multiple pathways for students to demonstrate their mastery and growth.

Dismantling Educational Apartheid

The brighter future we envision for Black students rejects the notion that zip code should determine educational quality (Rothstein, 2017). It challenges the resource disparities that have historically underfunded schools in Black communities while recognizing that throwing money at broken systems isn't enough—we need fundamental transformation. Community-controlled schools emerge where local families have real power in decision-making about curriculum, teaching methods, and resource allocation. These schools become anchor institutions that strengthen neighborhoods while preparing students for success in any environment they choose to enter. Moreover, technology becomes a bridge that connects under-resourced schools with excellent teachers, advanced courses, and global learning opportunities. But this technology serves community values rather than replacing human connection and cultural grounding.

Our Vision for Learning Communities

The future we envision builds upon the village-raising-a-child wisdom that has sustained Black families through centuries of challenge and triumph. These learning communities recognize that education is fundamentally about preparing young people to contribute to their communities while pursuing their individual dreams, using six community-related approaches.

Extended Family Learning Networks. Just as Black families have always understood that parenting is a communal responsibility, future learning communities operate on the principle that teaching is too important to be left to individual teachers working in isolation. Instead, children learn from networks of caring adults who each contribute their unique knowledge and perspective. Children studying mathematics might work with their teacher during school hours, receive tutoring from an engineer aunt after school, practice problem-solving with grandparents who share stories of how they used math in their daily lives, and participate in weekend math circles led by community college students. This network ensures that learning is reinforced across multiple relationships and contexts. These networks also provide multiple mentors and role models, so every child sees pathways to success that resonate with their interests and aspirations. The basketball coach becomes a physics teacher when explaining trajectory and momentum. The church organist becomes a mathematics instructor when exploring musical scales and rhythms. The community activist becomes a social studies teacher when discussing systems change and civic engagement.

Intergenerational Wisdom Sharing. Black communities have long been intergenerational spaces in which elders are revered for their wisdom and young people are valued for their energy and fresh perspectives. Future learning communities intentionally create opportunities for intergenerational exchange. High school students might interview elderly community members about their experiences during the civil rights movement, creating oral history projects that preserve important stories while developing research and communication skills. Middle school students might teach senior citizens about technology while learning patience and communication skills. Elementary students might help tend community gardens alongside elderly neighbors while studying plant biology and nutrition. These intergenerational connections provide young people with wisdom and perspective that can't be found in textbooks while giving older adults a sense of purpose and connection. They also strengthen community bonds and ensure that cultural knowledge is passed down through generations.

Culturally Responsive Innovation Hubs. The learning communities we envision become centers of innovation where students use cutting-edge technology and contemporary methods to address age-old challenges facing Black communities. These are not separate, distinct programs or special initiatives; rather, they are integral to how learning occurs.

Students studying computer science might develop apps that help small businesses in their neighborhoods manage inventory or connect with customers. Those learning biology might research health disparities in their communities and design interventions. Students exploring media arts might create documentaries that challenge stereotypes and celebrate community strengths. These innovation hubs recognize that Black students aren't just consumers of technology and knowledge—they're creators and inventors who can use their education to solve problems and build solutions that serve their communities.

Healing-Centered Learning Environments

The future learning communities we envision recognize that many Black students carry trauma from historical and contemporary racism, and that healing must be integrated into education rather than treated as a separate issue (Ginwright, 2018). These environments are designed to be therapeutic without being clinical, supportive without being condescending. Mindfulness practices drawn from African traditions become part of daily routines. Conflict-resolution skills grounded in restorative justice principles are taught and practiced. Art, music, and movement are used as both learning tools and healing modalities. Community circles provide space for students to process experiences and build connections (Jagers et al., 2025). These healing-centered approaches do not lower academic expectations. Instead, they create the emotional safety that allows students to take the intellectual risks necessary for deep learning. When students feel seen, valued, and supported, they are more likely to engage fully in challenging academic work.

Community-Accountable Assessment

Instead of relying solely on standardized tests that often fail to capture the full range of student learning, future learning communities develop assessment systems that are accountable to the communities they serve without lowering academic expectations. These systems measure not just individual academic growth but also community contribution, cultural knowledge, and social-emotional development. Student portfolios include academic work alongside community service projects, creative expressions, leadership experiences, and reflections on personal growth. Community members participate in portfolio reviews, celebrating student achievements and providing feedback that connects learning to real-world application (Maier et al., 2017). These assessment approaches recognize that the ultimate measure of educational success isn't just whether students can pass tests, but whether they're prepared to contribute meaningfully to their communities and pursue their dreams with confidence and competence.

Economic Justice Through Education

The learning communities we envision understand that education without economic opportunity is incomplete. They create pathways that lead not just to college but to career success, entrepreneurship, and community wealth-building. High school students do not just learn about economics—they start businesses, participate in cooperative enterprises, and develop financial literacy that will serve them throughout their lives. They examine the history of Black business development and analyze contemporary examples of community-controlled economic development. These communities also recognize that not every student will or should follow the college-prep pathway. They create respected pathways into skilled trades, creative industries, and entrepreneurship that build individual wealth while strengthening the economic foundations of communities.

The Path Forward: From Vision to Reality

As opposed to transformation through policy mandates or top-down initiatives, real, meaningful, and lasting educational transformation or change will spring from the grassroots efforts of Black families, educators, and community members who refuse to accept the educational status quo and commit to creating alternatives that honor their children's full humanity.

Starting Where We Are. Every parent who supplements their child's education with cultural knowledge, every teacher who brings Black history and achievements into their daily lessons, every community member who volunteers as a mentor or tutor is already contributing to this transformation. The future we envision builds on these existing efforts and connects them into a more comprehensive network of support. In the same way, churches, community centers, libraries, and other existing institutions become partners in this educational transformation. After-school programs incorporate academic support with cultural education. Summer programs combine skill-building with community service. Weekend workshops bring families together for shared learning experiences.

Policy That Serves Community Vision

While this transformation is fundamentally a grassroots movement, supportive policies can accelerate progress. Community-controlled school initiatives, increased funding for culturally responsive curricula, and support for alternative teacher certification programs that recruit educators from the communities they serve all contribute to the changes we envision. But policy must follow community vision rather than lead it. The most important changes happen when communities organize to demand better education for their children and then work to create it themselves.

Building the Village We Need

The African proverb tells us it takes a village to raise a child, but we must also acknowledge that in many places, the village has been scattered or weakened by systemic racism and economic displacement. Part of our educational work involves rebuilding the villages our children need to thrive. This means creating learning communities that extend beyond school walls to include families, neighbors, local businesses, faith communities, and cultural organizations. It entails recognizing that everyone in the community has something to teach and something to learn. It also means understanding that raising a classroom—creating an educational environment where all children can flourish—requires the same collective commitment that our ancestors brought to raising children. It requires the same wisdom, the same love, and the same determination to ensure that the next generation surpasses the achievements of the previous one.

A Future Worthy of Our Children

The educational future we envision is not merely to boost test scores or increase graduation rates, though those outcomes will follow naturally from our deeper transformation. In a broader sense, the educational future for our children depends on creating learning environments that honor the full humanity of Black children, build on the strengths they bring from their communities, and prepare them to lead in whatever fields they choose to pursue. This future recognizes that Black children are not problems to be solved but gifts to be celebrated, not deficits to be remediated but assets to be developed, not empty vessels to be filled but bright flames to be nurtured. When we center Black family wisdom in education, we do significantly more than improve outcomes for Black children—we create more joyful, more effective, more humane learning environments for all children. The village that raises the classroom benefits everyone in it. The future then is not something that happens to us; it is something we create together, one child at a time, one family at a time, one community at a time. And when we build it with the wisdom our ancestors have always known, that future will be worthy of the dreams they held for us and the dreams we hold for the generations yet to come.

Let us ensure that our children become the wildest dreams of future generations, educated in the fullness of their brilliance and prepared to transform the world.

We are the ones we have been waiting for. — **June Jordan**

CONCLUSION: THE JOURNEY CONTINUES

"We who believe in freedom cannot rest until it comes." — **Ella Baker**

Bringing It All Together

We began this journey with a simple yet profound truth: it takes a village to raise a child, and it takes that same village to raise a classroom. This text argues that Black family wisdom—passed down through generations of struggle, survival, and triumph—offers the keys to transforming education not just for Black children but for all children who have been underserved by systems that fail to recognize their full humanity. And, this wisdom is not new: It is as old as the first enslaved grandmother who taught her grandchildren to read in secret, as enduring as the teachers who walked miles to one-room schoolhouses, as powerful as the parents who integrated hostile schools because they believed in their children's right to learn. What is new is our collective commitment to centering this wisdom in educational spaces that have too often dismissed it as irrelevant or insufficient.

The Threads That Bind

Throughout our exploration, several threads have woven themselves through every chapter, creating a tapestry of understanding that reveals the interconnected nature of community-based education:

Relationship as Foundation. Every transformative educational experience we've examined has been rooted in authentic relationships between learners and their communities. When children see themselves reflected in their teachers, when families feel genuinely welcomed into educational spaces, when community members are valued as knowledge holders, learning becomes more than an academic exercise—it becomes an act of love and resistance.

Cultural Wealth as Curriculum. We have seen how the knowledge systems that live in Black families and communities—from mathematical concepts embedded in double-dutch rope jumping to scientific principles demonstrated in hair braiding patterns. These are not just supplementary resources but essential components of rigorous education. When schools honor and build upon this cultural wealth, they do not lower standards; they raise them by recognizing the full spectrum of human intelligence.

Collective Responsibility. The village approach to education holds that every adult in a child's community shares responsibility for the child's learning and development. This is not just about volunteer hours or fundraising; ultimately, it is about recognizing that when any child in our community struggles, we all struggle, and when any child succeeds, we all celebrate that victory.

Healing as Learning. Black children often carry the weight of historical and contemporary trauma, but they also carry the strength and resilience that enabled their ancestors to survive and thrive. Educational environments that integrate healing with learning do not coddle students; they instead create the emotional safety necessary for children to take the intellectual risks that deep learning requires.

Critical Consciousness. Perhaps most importantly, we recognize that education grounded in Black family wisdom naturally develops critical consciousness, giving our children the ability to analyze systems, question inequities, and work toward justice, preparing them, in the final analysis, for citizenship in a democracy that requires engaged, thoughtful participants. These threads, rather than existing in isolation, are interwoven into the daily practices of families who gather around kitchen tables to help with homework while sharing stories of their own educational journeys. They are present in churches where children learn public speaking through youth programs and develop leadership skills through community service. They are alive in barbershops and beauty salons, where informal mentoring occurs alongside casual conversation, and in community gardens, where lessons in biology and environmental science grow alongside vegetables and flowers.

A Love Letter to Learners and Educators

To Our Children: The Inheritors of Dreams

Dear ones, you who sit in classrooms where your brilliance isn't always recognized, you who carry the dreams of ancestors who couldn't imagine the opportunities before you today—this work is for you. You are not broken. You do not need to be fixed. You are not empty vessels waiting to be filled with someone else's knowledge. You are inheritors of centuries of wisdom, carriers of cultural wealth, and creators of tomorrow's solutions.

When the world tells you that your way of speaking is not academic enough, prove them wrong by mastering the English language and co-switching between the standard and cultural dialects as you choose to, remembering that your ancestors transformed the English language into poetry, turning the oppressor's tongue into liberation songs. When standardized tests suggest you are not smart enough, remember that your great-grandparents created mathematical systems to navigate the Underground Railroad and developed communication networks that connected communities across hundreds of miles. Always remember that your questions are not disruptions—they are genuine expressions of critical thinking; that your need for movement is not an indication of disorder. Instead, it is kinesthetic intelligence. Your loyalty to family and community is a measure of true success, including those you love, rather than a distraction from individual achievement.

The village that raised you includes not only your biological family but also every teacher who recognized your potential, every neighbor who checked on your well-being, and every community member who shared their knowledge with you. You are the product of their collective love, and you carry their hopes into every classroom you enter. Learn everything you can. Master every skill. But never forget that your education is incomplete until you use it to lift others as you climb. The degrees you earn, the careers you build, the innovations you create all mean more when they serve the liberation of your people and the healing of your community.

To Our Families: The First and Forever Teachers

Dear mothers and fathers, grandparents and guardians, aunts and uncles who have always known that education begins at home, your knowledge matters. Your experiences are a valid curriculum. Your expectations for your children's success are not overly high, but they are precisely what's needed to counter a world that often expects too little.

You have been teaching your children since before they could speak, showing them how to navigate multiple worlds, how to code-switch when necessary while maintaining their authentic selves, and how to excel academically while staying rooted in community values. This is sophisticated pedagogy that most professional educators struggle to master.

Remember that when you advocate for your children in school settings, you are not being difficult—you're being protective. When you supplement their education with cultural knowledge, you are not undermining their teachers, but you are ensuring they receive a complete education. When you maintain high expectations while providing emotional support, you are being loving rather than contradictory.

Do not ever let anyone convince you that your involvement in your children's education is unwelcome or unnecessary: you know your children better than any standardized test; you understand their learning styles, their interests, their challenges, and their potential better than any external assessment. Therefore, trust your knowledge and continue to be your children's first and most important advocates.

To Our Educators: The Bridge Builders

Dear teachers, administrators, counselors, and support staff who have chosen to dedicate your lives to nurturing young minds, thank you. Your work is sacred, your impact immeasurable, and your challenges real. We see you staying late to provide extra support, spending your own money on classroom supplies, and carrying students' struggles home with you.

Whether you share your students' cultural background or come from different communities, you have the power to honor the wisdom that children bring from their families and neighborhoods. You can be the bridge between home and school cultures, helping students recognize that they need not choose between academic success and cultural authenticity. Empowering our children does not require you to become someone you are not or to pretend you understand experiences you have not lived; it requires you to approach your students with genuine curiosity about their lives, respect for their families' knowledge, and commitment to creating learning environments where every child can thrive.

When you incorporate call-and-response into your teaching methods, you are being more culturally responsive without sacrificing rigor. When you allow students to work collaboratively, you are honoring learning styles that have served African communities for millennia; this approach does not, in any way, make things easier. When you integrate social justice themes into your curriculum, you are making the subject meaningful and relevant, not political.

Remember that your students' success is not separate from their community's success. When you invest in one child, you are investing in an entire network of relationships that will benefit from that child's growth. When you partner with families rather than simply informing them, you multiply your impact exponentially.

To Our Communities: The Village That Raises

Dear community members, faith leaders, business owners, elders, and neighbors who understand that children's success is everyone's responsibility, your participation is essential. Education cannot be relegated to schools alone. It requires the engagement of entire communities working together with shared purpose and mutual respect. Your experiences are textbooks waiting to be opened. Your businesses are classrooms where real-world learning happens. Your stories are history lessons that bring the past to life. Your challenges are problems that students can help solve while developing critical thinking skills.

When you mentor a young person, you are not just helping one child— you're modeling for other adults how to invest in the next generation. When you share your knowledge with students, you're not just teaching— you're preserving cultural wisdom that might otherwise be lost. When you advocate for better educational resources in your community, you're not just complaining—you're exercising democratic citizenship.

The village that raises a classroom extends far beyond school walls. It includes every space where children learn and grow: homes and churches, community centers and libraries, parks and businesses, barbershops and beauty salons. Every adult in these spaces has the potential to be an educator, and every interaction can be a learning opportunity.

The Unfinished Work of Community Learning

As we conclude this exploration of Black family wisdom in education, we must acknowledge that our work remains incomplete. The transformation we have envisioned requires ongoing commitment from all of us—learners, families, educators, and community members working together across generations.

The Ongoing Struggle for Educational Justice. Despite decades of civil rights activism and educational reform efforts, significant disparities persist in educational outcomes between Black students and their peers. These disparities are not the result of cultural deficits or family failures; they are the predictable outcomes of systemic inequities that have been centuries in the making.

Addressing these inequities requires more than good intentions or surface-level diversity initiatives. It requires fundamental changes in how we fund schools, train teachers, design curricula, and measure success. It requires honest conversations about racism and its impact on educational systems. It requires sustained activism from families and communities who refuse to accept inadequate education for their children.

This work is necessarily political because education is inherently political. The question is not whether we should inject politics into education: it is whether we will acknowledge the political nature of educational decisions and work to ensure they serve justice rather than perpetuate inequality.

Building Bridges Across Difference. One of the most important aspects of our unfinished work involves building bridges across racial, economic, and cultural differences. The village approach to education does not mean creating separate systems for different groups. Instead, it means creating inclusive systems that honor all families' wisdom while working toward shared goals of student success and community wellbeing. Building bridges requires having difficult conversations and uncomfortable reckonings: It means white educators and families examining their own cultural assumptions and recognizing the ways they may have unintentionally perpetuated harm. It means that middle-class families across backgrounds recognize that their children's success is linked to that of children from low-income families. It means communities working together to address the root causes of educational inequality rather than simply treating symptoms. Building these bridges to eliminate differences or pretend we are all the same. Rather, it is about creating spaces in which differences are valued as sources of strength and learning rather than as barriers to overcome.

Sustaining the Movement. Educational transformation is not a destination but a journey that requires sustained commitment across generations. The changes we have described in this book will not happen overnight, and they certainly will not happen without continuous effort from all of us. This means supporting organizations and initiatives that are already doing this work in communities across the country. It means voting for policies and candidates who prioritize educational equity. It entails ongoing conversations about education within our families, faith communities, and neighborhood organizations.

Most importantly, it means raising a generation of young people who understand that their education is not just about individual advancement but about collective liberation. These young people will face challenges we can't imagine and will need to continue the work of transformation in ways we haven't yet envisioned.

The Ripple Effects

When we center Black family wisdom in education, the benefits extend far beyond Black children and families. The collaborative learning methods, culturally responsive teaching practices, and community engagement strategies that serve Black students well also benefit students from other underserved communities: The critical thinking skills that develop when students examine systemic inequities prepare all students to be more thoughtful citizens. The social-emotional learning that happens in healing-centered classrooms helps all children develop empathy and resilience. Community partnerships that bring real-world relevance to academic learning engage students more deeply in their education.

Bringing about the kind of change that results in effective learning and powerful empowerment is not about creating special programs for Black students or lowering standards to accommodate cultural differences. It is ultimately about raising standards for all students by recognizing and building on the full range of human intelligence and cultural knowledge in our communities.

The Long Arc of History

We are part of a long historical arc that bends toward justice but requires constant effort to maintain its trajectory. Our ancestors who learned to read by candlelight, who walked miles to attend school, who faced down mobs to integrate classrooms did this work not so we could become comfortable with the status quo. Oh no! They did it so we could continue pushing toward full educational equity for all children.

Every time we advocate for a child who is being underserved, we honor their sacrifice. Every time we create learning environments that celebrate cultural diversity, we build on their foundation. Every time we refuse to accept inadequate education as inevitable, we advance their vision of liberation through learning. The work continues because the dream of educational equity remains unfulfilled. But we have more tools, more knowledge, and more allies than previous generations. We also have their example of how ordinary people can create extraordinary change when they work together with shared purpose and unwavering commitment.

A Covenant for the Future

As I close this book, I invite you to enter into a covenant—a sacred agreement between all of us who believe that every child deserves an education that honors their full humanity and prepares them to contribute to the healing of our world.

We invoke this covenant to see every child as brilliant, regardless of how their brilliance is expressed or measured. We covenant to honor the wisdom that families bring to educational settings, even when that wisdom doesn't match traditional academic expectations. We covenant to work toward educational systems that serve all children well, understanding that this requires dismantling systems that currently serve some children at the expense of others.

We employ this covenant to remember that education is not neutral—it either functions as the practice of freedom or as the practice of domination. We choose freedom. We aim to create learning environments in which every child can discover their gifts, develop their potential, and understand their responsibility to use their education to serve justice and community well-being.

We embrace this covenant to support one another in this work, recognizing that none of us can transform education alone, but all of us together can create change that seemed impossible just a generation ago. We covenant to celebrate small victories while maintaining our commitment to larger transformation.

Most importantly, we faithfully commit ourselves to this covenant to continue this work beyond the pages of this book, beyond the workshops and conferences where we discuss these ideas, beyond the moments of inspiration that brought us to this movement. We covenant to make this work part of our daily lives, family conversations, community engagement, and ongoing commitment to justice.

The Circle Remains Unbroken

In African American tradition, the circle represents continuity, connection, and the eternal cycle of learning that flows from one generation to the next. As this book ends, we do not end; we simply complete one turn of the circle before beginning another. The elders who shared their wisdom throughout these pages pass it on to us. We add our own experiences and insights before passing it on to the young people who

will carry this work forward. They will face new challenges and discover new solutions, but they will build upon the
foundation we've laid together.

The village that raises a classroom is not a fixed entity but a living, breathing community that grows and changes while maintaining its core commitment to nurturing every child. You are part of this village now. Your voice matters. Your experience contributes to our collective wisdom. Your actions shape the future of education for generations to come. The journey continues not because we haven't reached our destination, but because the destination itself keeps expanding as we grow in our understanding of what's possible when we center love, justice, and community wisdom in educational settings.

We are awakening to new possibilities for education, new ways of honoring the wisdom that exists in all our communities, new methods of preparing young people for a future that will require both academic excellence and cultural grounding, both individual achievement and collective commitment. The village that raises a classroom is not just a metaphor—it's a way of life that we're building together, one relationship at a time, one child at a time, one community at a time. The journey continues, and we continue it together. *Asé. May it be so.*

The village that raised us calls us to raise the village. The classroom that taught us calls us to teach. The love that sustained us calls us to sustain love. The journey continues, and we travel it together. **– Dr. Krystal L. Clemons**

REFERENCES

Anderson, J. D. (1988). *The education of Blacks in the South, 1860–1935.* University of North Carolina Press.

Annamma, S. A. (2017). *The pedagogy of pathologization: Dis/abled girls of color in the school-prison nexus.* Routledge.

Annamma, S. A., Ferri, B. A., & Connor, D. J. (2018). Disability critical race theory: Exploring the intersectional lineage, emergence, and potential futures of DisCrit in education. *Review of Research in Education, 42(1), 46-71.*

Anyon, Y., Gregory, A., Stone, S., Farrar, J., Jenson, J. M., McQueen, J., Downing, B., Greer, E. & Simmons, J. (2016). Restorative interventions and school discipline sanctions in a large urban school district. *American Educational Research Journal, 53(6),* 1663–1697.

Aylward, B. S., Gal-Szabo, D. E., & Taraman, S. (2021). Racial, ethnic, and sociodemographic disparities in diagnosis of autism spectrum disorder. *JAMA Network Open, 4(8),* e2116024. https://doi.org/10.1001/jamanetworkopen.2021.16024

Carter Andrews, D. J., Brown, T., Castro, E., & Id-Deen, E. (2019). The impossibility of being "perfect and white": Black girls' racialized and gendered schooling experiences. *American Educational Research Journal, 56(6), 2531-2572.*

Clemons, K. L., & Johnson, K. F. (2019). African American pastors and their perceptions of professional school counseling. *The Journal of Negro Education, 88(4),* 467–478.

Clemons, K. L., & Cokley, R. K. (2022). "There Isn't a Racist Bone in My Body!": A Case Study on Fostering Anti-Racism in School Counseling. *In Developing anti-racist practices in the helping professions: Inclusive theory, pedagogy, and application* (pp. 329-360). Cham: Springer Nature Switzerland

Clemons, K. L. (2024). It takes a village: A conceptual model for Black American community partnerships. *Professional School Counseling, 28(1)*, *https://doi.org/10.1177/2156759X231225222*

Clemons, K. L., & Mayes, R. D. (2024). Twice-exceptional Black girls: A case study in early childhood. *Perspectives on Early Childhood Psychology and Education, 8(1), 6.*

Coker, T. R., Elliott, M. N., Toomey, S. L., Schwebel, D. C., Cuccaro, P., Emery, S. T., Davies, S. L., Visser, S. N., & Schuster, M. A. (2016). Racial and ethnic disparities in ADHD diagnosis and treatment. *Pediatrics, 138(3), e20160407.* https://doi.org/10.1542/peds.2016-0407

Connor, D. J., Ferri, B. A., & Annamma, S. A. (2021). From the personal to the global: Engaging with and enacting DisCrit theory across multiple spaces. *Journal of Race, Ethnicity and Education, 24(6),* 857–872. https://doi.org/10.1080/13613324.2021.1918400

Crenshaw, K. W. (1989). Demarginalizing the intersection of race and sex: A Black feminist critique of antidiscrimination doctrine, feminist theory and antiracist politics. *University of Chicago Legal Forum, 1989(1),* 139-167.

Crosby, S. D., Howell, P., & Thomas, S. (2018). Social justice education through trauma-informed teaching. *Middle School Journal, 49(4)*, 15-23.

Davison, M., Penner, A., Penner, E., Pharris-Ciurej, N., Porter, S. R., Rose, E., Shem-Tov, Y, & Yoo, P. (2021). School Discipline and Racial Disparities in Early Adulthood. *EdWorkingPaper No. 21-434.* Annenberg Institute for School Reform at Brown University.

DeMatthews, D. E. (2020). Addressing racism and ableism in schools: A DisCrit leadership framework for principals. *The Educational Forum, 84(1),* 21–39. https://doi.org/10.1080/00098655.2019.1690419

Dwyer, P. (2022). The neurodiversity approach(es): What are they and what do they mean for researchers? *Human Development, 66(2),* 73–92. https://doi.org/10.1159/000523723

Engram Jr., F. V. (2023). *Black liberation through action and resistance: MOVE.* Lexington Books.

Fadus, M. C., Ginsburg, K. R., Sobowale, K., & Halliday-Boykins, C. A. (2020). Unconscious bias and the diagnosis of disruptive behavior disorders and ADHD in African American and Hispanic youth. *Academic Psychiatry, 44(1),* 95–102. https://doi.org/10.1007/s40596-019-01127-6

Freire, P. (2020). Pedagogy of the oppressed. In Toward a sociology of education (pp. 374-386). Routledge.

Gay, G. (2018). *Culturally responsive teaching: Theory, research, and practice (3rd ed.).* Teachers College Press.

Ginwright, S. (2015). *Hope and healing in urban education: How urban activists and teachers are reclaiming matters of the heart.* Routledge.

Ginwright, S. (2018*). The future of healing: Shifting from trauma informed care to healing centered engagement. Occasional paper, 25, 25-32.*

González, N., Moll, L. C., & Amanti, C. (Eds.). (2005). *Funds of knowledge: Theorizing practices in households, communities, and classrooms.* Lawrence Erlbaum Associates Publishers.

Gregory, A., Clawson, K., Davis, A., & Gerewitz, J. (2016). The promise of restorative practices to transform teacher-student relationships and achieve equity in school discipline. *Journal of Educational and Psychological Consultation, 26(4),* 325-353.

Habayeb, S., Dababnah, S., Alshahrani, A., & Bakaeen, F. (2021). Still left behind: Fewer Black school-aged youth receive autism spectrum disorder diagnoses. *Journal of Autism and Developmental Disorders, 51,* 4408–4417.

Hatton, C. E., & Clemons, K. L. (2022). School counselors as social justice advocates: dismantling racism and bias in schools. *In Developing, Delivering, and Sustaining School Counseling Practices Through a Culturally Affirming Lens (pp. 76-96).* IGI Global Scientific Publishing.

Howard, T. C. (2019). *Why race and culture matter in schools: Closing the achievement gap in America's classrooms. (2ⁿᵈ ed).* Teachers College Press.

Jagers, R. J., Rivas-Drake, D., & Williams, B. (2025). Transformative social and emotional learning (SEL): Toward SEL in service of educational equity and excellence. *In Social and Emotional Learning (pp. 39-62).* Routledge.

Jeynes, W. H. (2016). A meta-analysis: The relationship between parental involvement and African American school outcomes. *Journal of Black Studies, 47 (3), 195-216.* https://doi.org/10.1177/0021934715623522

Kendi, I. X. (2016). *Stamped from the beginning: The definitive history of racist ideas in America.* Nation Books.

Leadbitter, K., Buckle, K. L., Ellis, C., & Dekker, M. (2021). Autistic self-advocacy and the neurodiversity movement. *Frontiers in Psychology, 12, 635690.* https://doi.org/10.3389/fpsyg.2021.635690

Lester, A. M., Chow, J. C., & Melton, T. N. (2020). Quality is critical for meaningful synthesis of afterschool program effects: A systematic review and meta-analysis. *Journal of Youth and Adolescence, 49(2),* 369–382.

Lincoln, C. E., & Mamiya, L. H. (1990). *The Black church in the African American experience.* Duke University Press.

Love, B. L. (2019). *We want to do more than survive: Abolitionist teaching and the pursuit of educational freedom.* Beacon Press.

Maier, A., Daniel, J., Oakes, J., & Lam, L. (2017). *Community schools as an effective school improvement strategy.* Learning Policy Institute.

Morris, E. W. (2016). *Pushout: The criminalization of Black girls in schools.* New Press.

Nasir, N. S., Givens, J., & Chatmon, C. (Eds.). (2019). *We dare say love: Supporting the educational life of Black boys.* Teachers College Press.

Nasir, N., Lee, C. D., Pea, R., & McKinney de Royston, M. (Eds.). (2020). *Handbook of the cultural foundations of learning. Routledge.*

Overstreet, S., & Chafouleas, S. M. (2016). Trauma-informed schools: Introduction to the special issue. *School Mental Health, 8(1)*, 1–6.

Paris, D., & Alim, H. S. (2017). *Culturally sustaining pedagogies: Teaching and learning for justice in a changing world.* Teachers College Press.

Parker, J. S. (2021). School mental health services and predominantly Black churches. *The Journal of Negro Education, 90(4)*, 508–523.

Parker, J. S., Haskins, N., Whitehead, R. A., Christian, B., Jackson, T., & Ford, A. (2025). Black youth access to mental and behavioral health care and academic support through e-mentoring and a Black church partnership. *School Mental Health, 17(1)*, 73–89.

Pham, H. H., Daniels, J., Shea, M., & Mandell, D. S. (2022). Racial and ethnic differences in rates and age of autism spectrum disorder diagnosis, 2017–2021. *JAMA Network Open, 5(10)*, e2236922.

Ross, L. C. (2016). *The divine nine: The history of African American fraternities and sororities.* Kensington.

Rothstein, R. (2017). *The color of law: A forgotten history of how our government segregated America.* Liveright Publishing.

Shi, Y., Hunter Guevara, L. R., Dykhoff, H. J., Sangaralingham, L. R., Phelan, S. M., Zaccariello, M. J., Shah, N. D., & Moriarty, J. P. (2021). Racial disparities in diagnosis of attention-deficit/hyperactivity disorder in a US national sample. *JAMA Network Open, 4(3)*, e210321. *https://doi.org/10.1001/jamanetworkopen.2021.0321*

Waitoller, F. R., & Thorius, K. A. K. (2016). Cross-pollinating culturally sustaining pedagogy and universal design for learning. *Harvard Educational Review, 86(3)*, 366–389. https://doi.org/10.17763/1943-5045-86.3.366

Warren, M. R., Hong, S., Rubin, C. L., & Uy, P. S. (2009). Beyond the bake sale: A community-based relational approach to parent engagement in schools. *Teachers College Record, 111(9)*, 2209–2254.

Watkins, W. H. (2001). *The white architects of Black education.* Teachers College Press.

Woodson, C. G. (1933). *The mis-education of the Negro*. Associated Publishers.

Yosso, T. J. (2005). Whose culture has capital? A critical race theory discussion of community cultural wealth. *Race Ethnicity and Education, 8(1),* 69–91.